Spent

My accidental career in retail

Dana Goldstein

Keep doing
the good work!

Dana G

For all the retail workers who put up with the worst of humanity, either through management or customers. I see you. You are doing a great job.

Contents

1

Doing Time

I'm no stranger to the penal system. When I was 11, I was caught slipping a family-size chocolate bar up my sleeve while in a drugstore. I was aware of the man watching me, tailing me through the store, but had no idea he was an undercover security guard. As I tried to leave, he grabbed me by the arm, took me to the basement and told me I was in a heap of trouble. He threatened me, saying the store might press charges and the police might have to get involved. The poor soul had no idea he was dealing with a sassy latchkey kid who was more afraid of her mother than any authorities. I refused to give him a phone number to contact my mother, choosing instead to give him my grandparents' phone number. They came from the other end of the city to get me, profusely apologized to the store manager, and assured him that I would not set foot in his store ever again.

But of course I did. I let an acceptable length of time pass before I was back there, shoplifting bags of caramels and packs of gum. On my third visit, I scanned the aisles for the security guard, but he wasn't there anymore. I kept my eyes peeled for the manager, but I never saw him on the sales floor.

I now know this is typical for retail. It's a twisted world where no good deed goes unpunished and managers stay behind locked doors.

Working in retail is harsh. It's a world where cutbacks are commonplace and managers fight for scraps, always paring back to stay within the payroll percentages to appease the Wall Street or Bay Street investors. When you enter the world of retail as an employee, you can expect your vision of helping people and easy work to be clouded by, well, people.

I'm confident that almost everyone you know has worked some kind of retail job. It's a rite of passage from childhood into adulthood; the bridge between living by your parents' rules and discovering the rules of real life. That first paycheque is significant, even if the dollar value isn't. My first paycheque meant I could finally buy the things I had coveted my whole teen life: a Benetton rugby shirt, Tretorn running shoes, and a burger and fries at the greasy dive down the road from my high school. There was power in my purse.

But working in retail comes at a price, especially as a teenager. Weekends and evenings are no longer your own. Your friends without jobs go to the pool while you sweat out the summer in your polyester uniform. You smell like hamburgers or dry cleaning solution, and that will be all you can smell some days. Your work shoes can never cross the threshold of your home because they are always slimy or sticky and you can't figure out why because you work in a clothing store.

I never intended to be employed in the retail sector beyond my university years. My aspirations went further than stocking shelves, folding towels, and making popcorn. After the allure of babysitting had run its course, I landed my first retail job in 1985 at an amusement park. I was 15 and thought retail was a career for people who didn't do well in school. But when, in 1990, a recession swept across Canada and the United States, forcing people out of long-held careers and into retail to make ends meet, I realized these jobs were the foundation of the economy. For two years, while I was still safely cocooned in university and a part-time job at a bank, people from all walks of life were looking for work wherever they could find it.

I've worked in so many different retail environments, some of which enriched me, but most of them chipped away at my soul. I've had access to backrooms, back offices, and the backstabbing common among managers. I've pored over financial books, look-books, and books on the psychology of shopping.

Ask anyone who has spent more than a smattering of evenings and weekends in retail, and they'll refer to how much time they did, like they've served a prison sentence. It's a shitty environment to work in. Upper management is filled with power-tripping assholes who wield performance reviews like police batons (and will metaphorically beat you over the head with one). Customers will treat you and the merchandise like garbage, piling and dropping things wherever they please, knowing it's part of your job to clean up after them. You are a second-class citizen.

As a retail manager, I dealt with employees stealing, colleagues having affairs, broke customers who maxed out credit cards trying to buy happiness, bosses who couldn't spell, and bosses who put company policy above humanity. I had a general manager who whined, daily, about how her boyfriend was never going to leave his wife and one who thought it was okay to clip his fingernails in the lunchroom. But I've also had stellar managers who taught me how to be a better manager.

I spent more than a decade in retail, and in all that time I met only two people who deliberately chose this career path. They never intended to stay in the store, but had loftier goals, their sights set on corporate jobs at head office. Staff work where it's geographically convenient, while management goes wherever we are sent. The retail world is small and turnover is a huge problem. At one point in my retail career, I had hired and fired so many people that I started recognizing them in interviews when I moved to a new company.

I collected valuable life lessons while I sold blue jeans, built schedules, and managed inventory. My definition of retail includes the gambling industry because the lessons I learned there are too colourful not to share. If you've ever bought chocolate at the till of a bookstore, had anxiety dreams about stocking bath bombs where the hand soap should go, or watched a customer unravel over socks, this book is for you. We've all done time, one way or another.

2

It's in the Blood

On July 23, 1920, a 10-year-old boy stood at the railing on the deck of the SS Minnedosa, watching the work at the Liverpool dockyards. Icek Fruchtman was tired and nervous, weary from the first leg of his journey. He never imagined there could be so many places on the way to his new home. In the last six days, as his family fled Poland, they had sat in the back of a horse-drawn wagon and stood with strangers in the open carriage of a train. And then there was the walking. So much walking.

"This is for sure not the Orient Express," his older brother, Yankel, had said as the train rocked them like bowling pins.

"How would you know?" Icek challenged. Even though deep down he loved his brother, it was tiresome how he thought he was so smart.

"I read about it in a book. You know what those are, right?"

Icek fought the urge to punch Yankel. They were

hungry, dirty, and if they were being honest with themselves, a little scared.

"I'm not a *dummkopf*," Icek protested. "I know how to read. What's the Orient Express?"

"A fancy train. The people who wanted to kill Dracula took it."

Icek nodded. He remembered that book well. On the cover, a white-haired man in a cape was climbing down a wall.

Later, on the deck of the ship that would take them to Canada, Yankel and Icek stood side by side, united by the unknown. Their little brother Hymy was sitting on the wet deck, leaning against the back of Yankel's legs, trying to stay awake.

"Thank God we made it this far," Yankel said. Icek shook his head and rolled his eyes to the sky. He was already questioning the existence of God. What God would allow typhus to take both his parents, one after the other?

Icek was trying to imagine his future life. Who would be waiting for them when the ship docked in Quebec City? How would they get to Toronto? Icek, his brothers, uncle, and cousins had fled during the height of the Polish war with Russia, but not before he had witnessed the horrors of war: death, food shortages, displaced families, and rampant anti-Semitism. The new world across the ocean held the promise of freedom and adventure. Icek knew almost nothing about Canada, other than its climate was similar to Poland's, a number of his family members were already there and working, and the vague references that life could be better.

Seven days after boarding the Canadian Pacific Shipping Line's ocean liner, the Fruchtman boys landed in Quebec City with rings of dirt around their necks, the growl of hunger in their bellies, and a desire to build a new life.

Icek, who would grow up to become my grandfather, changed his name from the Polish Icek to the more anglicized Irving. He started his working life as a dressmaker and raincoat cutter. My grandmother, Sylvia, who sailed from Poland eight years after Icek as her uncle's adopted daughter, was a dutiful wife and mother. She took care of the home and spent her days with extended family, but she wanted more. When my grandparents opened their goods store on the main floor of the apartment building they were living in, my grandmother was proud of how far they had come. It was the 1970s and it was perfectly acceptable for women to be working outside of the home. Plus, it gave her something engaging to do once her daughter was grown, married, and about to have a child of her own.

The store sold sundry items, from candy to toilet paper and everything in between. The shelves held anything that an apartment dweller might want or need: fuses in case one burned out while simultaneously vacuuming the living room, toasting bread, and watching TV; a wide assortment of feather dusters, cleaning cloths, and Easy-Off oven cleaner; canned soup, canned beans, and canned saucy spaghetti.

My grandparents were equal partners in the business; the workload was shared and the pride of ownership was clear, even to me, whose earliest memory of that shop was being allowed to pick one treat on Fridays before they closed for Sabbath.

"You own all this?" I asked, looking around with wonder at the shelves full of all manner of foods and household stuff. I had just walked into the shop, and I was dwarfed by the rows of shelves in the middle of the space, the high shelves lining the walls, and the displays of candy bars at the front counter. I was amazed they had so much stuff, and more importantly, could let me pick whatever I wanted and not have to pay for it. This was a big deal to an eight-year-old.

Perched behind the cash register, my grandfather peered at me over the top of his thick-framed glasses and smiled. "Well, we still have to pay for everything, but we can keep the money from our sales. What would you like to have today? Chocolate? Chips? Candy?"

I was overwhelmed by the choices and the options. "Can you come down here in the middle of the night and take whatever you want?" I asked, picturing my grandmother coming down the elevator in her nightgown, unlocking the door, and grabbing a can of soup.

My grandfather nodded and was about to answer when the bell above the door rang and a customer walked up to the front counter to buy a pack of cigarettes. My grandmother appeared out of nowhere, grabbed the cigarettes, and rang up the sale.

"Do you need matches or a lighter?" she asked. "Lighters are a dime, matches are a penny." She didn't wait for his answer—she was already reaching for the matches.

"Sure, I'll take some matches," the customer answered.

That's how the business was built. One penny pack of matches at a time.

I was amazed that my grandmother was able to sell something that a customer didn't even ask for. She anticipated a need and introduced two options at two very different price points. It's like she knew that presenting the lower-cost matches at the end of her sentence would guarantee the sale. She was shrewd when it came to business, but she was smart enough to

9

not let it show too much. Running a variety store (or "tuck shop," as they called it) was hard work. The hours were always long, the margins were sometimes minimal. But this was their baby. If they wanted to sell high-margin pipes, they could put them front and centre. If they wanted to get rid of items that didn't move, they could mark them down. They could say yes and no as they pleased to salesmen offering new items. They relied on themselves for their paycheques. They got to know the names of their regular customers, who all lived in the three buildings the store served. They didn't call themselves entrepreneurs, they called themselves grocers.

My father's side of the family also had roots in

retail. My uncle—my father's brother-in-law—opened a chain of furniture stores in and around Toronto. A salesman to the core, my uncle orchestrated a publicity stunt that took him to Alaska in the 1960s to—as the old saying went—sell a refrigerator to an Eskimo. My father was a store manager at one of the many locations, eventually moving into a district manager role. My aunt started businesses out of boredom. My father ran a couple of them for their very short business lives until he decided to venture out on his own. He ran his citizens band (CB) two-way radio business out of the basement of his house. He wore all the hats: acquisition, distribution, shipping, and accounting. He worked long after everyone had gone to bed. He spent days on the road, selling and delivering six-foot antennas, radios, and an assortment of parts to ham radio enthusiasts, truckers, and hobbyists across southern Ontario. He gave me my first lessons in exceptional customer service.

Unlike my grandparents, who were energized by their work, my father seemed exhausted most of the time. I don't think he had passion for what he was selling, he was merely eking out a living. He built great relationships, but made poor choices. He would drive four hours to deliver a $50 product. He enjoyed meeting with customers, making every call in person last longer than it needed to. He would ship a single power cord overnight, paying more for the package than the value of its contents. Not the best business model.

I guess you could say I was born with sales in my blood. I could probably sell a swimsuit to a mermaid, but I wouldn't feel good about it. My conscience drives me, and that is something that is not welcomed or encouraged in retail. Rather than sell the swimsuit, I would send the mermaid to the best place I knew of where she could get reliable tail maintenance. I want to be helpful more than I want a commission. I value relationships with customers over knowing the sales figures. I watched my grandparents thrive, my uncle become a multi-millionaire, and my father toil for a few bucks. I subconsciously learned all I needed to know about running a business—a retail business specifically —just from watching my family. Still, when I landed my first retail job at the age of 15, I was sorely unprepared, really stupid, and made a horrible mistake.

3

You Never Forget Your First

"You should totally come with me and apply."

My best friend Audrey[1] was leaning against her locker, telling me why she was applying to spend a second spring and summer working at Canada's Wonderland. The amusement park just north of Toronto had opened four years earlier in 1981 and quickly became a playground and workplace of choice for teenagers from the Greater Toronto Area.

"It's sooo fun," she said. "Everyone who works there is, like, the same age as us. The money is okay, but you get to be outside and the supervisors are really cool. I joke around with them all the time. And, this is the best, you get into the park for free!"

I was intrigued but terrified at the same time. I had never applied for a job before. Apart from a few babysitting gigs, I had never been paid for any kind of work, never had an interview, never even set eyes on a job application. I had zero work experience, zero references, and zero confidence. But the lure of money, fun, and funnel cakes was too strong to ignore.

Audrey gave me the information: where to go, when to go, what to expect, what not to say, what to absolutely make sure I say, and gave me the lay of the land of the best departments to work for. Gaming is great, retail is good, stay away from food services and ride operations. I didn't ask why, I merely accepted her authority on the matter. She did, after all, have *experience.*

After Audrey convinced me to work there, I called the park to confirm what she had told me about when and how to apply. A hiring fair was happening over the coming weekend, they told me, and I could show up anytime between four o'clock Friday afternoon and six o'clock Sunday evening. This was 1985, before the internet and online applications made such things simple. The park wasn't easy to get to for a carless teen. I had to take a city bus, then the subway, then switch to a different bus system serving the outlying areas around the city.

Three days after the job fair, I was offered a job. I was to work the main gate—that's park lingo for working retail just inside the entrance to the park. I would be working the main store or at one of the carts scattered throughout the concourse. The concourse was a large open area near the front gates, which gave visitors a view of the fake mountain and the large fountains, making it the perfect place for guests to coordinate meeting at the end of the day or designating it as the place to meet should anyone get separated. Every visitor passed through the concourse—and all the opportunities to shop—on their way in and out of the park. I understand now that it was last-minute purchase persuasion at its best. All I knew back then was that it got really hot on that concourse.

I soon learned working a cart was the worst place to be in the height of a sweltering Toronto summer. There was only a tiny overhang roof, meant to shield the cash register display from the sun. I tested my contortionist capabilities trying to twist my body to fit under that useless overhang for respite. It was a wasted effort. My uniform of pantyhose, a full-length polyester skirt, and a balloon-sleeved blouse kept me warm and sweaty all summer long. The only good times to work the cart were early in the morning or for the closing shift, when the breezes were cool and the sun didn't cook you like a mini-cake in an Easy-Bake Oven.

The carts were no match for the action of the main store. Guests at the park were in and out all day long. When it rained, we sold loads of rain ponchos. When the temperature dropped after the rain stopped, we sold hundreds of sweatshirts. It was here, in the ebb and flow of consumerism, where a lifelong fascination with how people shop began.

Throughout the park, every department was its own micro-society. The ride operators tended to be older than me, mostly university students who drank too much and looked bored all day. The carnies—the ones operating the games—were really the fun bunch. They had parties and slept around with each other like the cast of one of the trashy prime-time dramas my mother loved to watch. Food services was dominated by pimple-faced kids, though I was never quite sure if the acne was caused by teenage hormones or by the sweaty, greasy conditions of their workplace.

Retail was a different breed altogether. For the first few weeks I was blissfully unaware of what kind of people I was working with. Once I started talking to my co-workers and spending time with them, I feared I had landed in a world of mischief. Main gate was the domain of pranksters, potheads, and thieves and I was way out of my element. I was a quiet girl who played by the rules. It was there, in my first real job, that I discovered so much more about myself.

I learned I was flexible and fluid and could fit into any group. I found it easy to find a place among every subset of co-workers. I could have had my choice of friends, but I made the decision to align with the thieves. My 15-year-old brain was amazed by all the "free" stuff we got. Along with my "friends," I pilfered the occasional T-shirt and sweatshirt, but the real benefit was found in working the cigarette counter. I stuck at least one pack per shift down my bra for my own consumption. I told myself that at least I wasn't as bad as Linda, who was stealing entire cartons and selling them at a discount to the other teens in her low-income high-rise apartment building.

Since Audrey and I worked in different departments and with schedules that didn't align, Linda became my closest friend, both at the park and outside of work. We hung out together on our days off, smoking stolen cigarettes and bumming around the Eaton Centre in downtown Toronto, talking big shit with our big hair and big shoulders, our frosted lips and our leg warmers. I always felt like she was scrutinizing me, assessing whether I was worth the effort friendship takes. Turns out my intuition was bang on. I would soon discover that ours was a friendship of convenience.

"You know how to void sales, right?" she asked me one night as we emerged from the movie theatre, having snuck in to see *Mad Max Beyond Thunderdome*.

"Of course." I nodded. "We were all trained on that."

"Yep, yep..." she agreed.

She was silent for a while as we walked to the food court. We had just hoovered large popcorns and large sodas, so we weren't looking for more food. Food courts in the '80s should have just been called flirt courts. They were filled with teenagers taking up tables, smoking, and talking stupid.

Once we had slid into the metal seats attached to the table, Linda leaned toward me like she had a secret.

"You know, if you void a cash sale, you can take the money and pocket it."

I blinked slowly, once, twice. My naïve brain was not understanding what she was saying.

"Don't I have to give the money back to the customer?"

Linda rolled her eyes.

"After they've gone. That's when you void and keep the money."

Heat travelled from my neck to my face. This was so dishonest and made me wildly uncomfortable. But it also set my heart racing. The thrill of theft was not new to me. The risk I took every time I pocketed a pack of smokes heightened, but my anxiety lessened with each shift I worked. There were so many of us behind the counter that it was nearly impossible to track who was doing what. But sticking my hand in the till was a different game. I wasn't sure I could pull it off without immense guilt. I thought about it for a day and a half and had made a decision by the time I worked my next shift. I would do this. If Linda could get away with it, so could I. I wanted to prove to myself—and to Linda— that guilt was temporary. I was going to try it. Once.

In my stupid, underdeveloped teenage brain, it never occurred to me that one void during a shift was normal, whereas five was cause for alarm. I also didn't consider that inventory was counted. If the cart was loaded with 12 pairs of sunglasses and six sold, simple math dictates there should be six left. If one sale was voided, there should be seven pairs nesting on the small spinner. After I got away with the first void, I was bold enough to try two. For almost three weeks, I skimmed money from the cash register. I kept track of my bank on a cash register receipt tucked into my bra. By the end of my shift, the ink was blurred by my cleavage sweat, but I could still figure out how much paper and how many coins would pad my B-cup. I shoved bills into the bottom of my shoes. I had to carefully disperse and tuck the coins under my breast, otherwise I would jingle like a belly dancer. It was a lot of effort for $40.74. Still, Linda and I laughed at how easy this was, how flush we were going to be with cash.

And then my world came crashing down.

At the end of one of our shifts, Linda and I sat on the floor in the main shop, legs spread, counting out the money in our cash drawers. I always balanced to the penny, even with the voids. This time, I had an overage of $22.73. I scraped my brain, trying to recall if I missed pulling any cash. At this point in my thievery, I had started to lose track of how many voids I was processing each shift. I looked around to see where the supervisors were. One was helping another cashier with her paperwork; one was walking in and out of the stockroom replenishing merchandise on the sales floor. I pulled out a twenty and a two-dollar bill and stuffed them in my bra. I pulled out the seventy-three cents and passed it to Linda, who added it to the pile of loose change she kept tucked up beside her leg, hidden from view. Whenever we worked together, we combined our change, swapped the coins out for bills and split it. She kept the extra coins because, she said, this whole thing was her idea. Occasionally, we left the pennies, thinking perfection every time was suspicious.

When I called my supervisor over to take my drawer to the back office, she checked everything, then signed off on my paperwork. I told Linda I'd wait for her at the bus stop in the employee parking lot. I made my way past the wood fencing separating the employee paths from the public areas of the park. It was a four-minute walk to the administrative building where all the offices were located, as well as the employee locker rooms. I knew this because you didn't want to miss the last bus out of the park and be stranded. It was vital to know how long it took to get there and change out of my uniform (seven minutes). The money in my shoe was getting sweaty, sliding forward because of my nylons and poking into my baby toe.

I passed the security guard standing just inside the fence, posted there to stop any visitors who might wander. He nodded and told me to have a good night. At the doors to the admin centre, I was greeted by a man and a woman I didn't know. The woman introduced herself, telling me she was from human resources. The man, she said, was from loss prevention.

I have no recollection of the conversation, but even after 35 years I can still remember the buzzing in my ears. I was sweating, and not just from the polyester of my uniform. In a blurred haze, I took off my shoes, revealing the damp and crumpled bills. I opened and emptied my locker, then dumped out the contents of my purse. Other staff came and went, all looking while trying not look to at what was happening. Linda came around the corner, flicked her eyes in my direction and walked right by me. I knew we were never going to speak to each other again. All my efforts at impressing her were for nothing.

I was permitted to change out of my uniform, and then taken to a boardroom where I was told I was being dismissed. After that, I heard only snippets: *too many voids, marked bills, immediate dismissal, no charges, no references.*

I was told I could leave. It was well past midnight and the last bus was long gone. In a daze, I walked to a payphone to call my mother and ask her to pick me up.

"It's late. Call your father," she snapped before hanging up on me. She hadn't even given me a chance to tell her what happened. My father had barely been a presence in my life, since my parents separated when I was two years old. I hardly knew my dad, outside the occasional Sunday visit.

I gently placed the handset back in its cradle. I opened my wallet to get another quarter. I didn't have one. Through my tears, I dug around in my purse, praying for a stray quarter. I searched my shoes, hoping a coin had slipped between the insole and the bottom of my shoe. I came up empty-handed. I looked around, hoping to see someone I knew, someone who could help me. There were a few cars still in the employee parking lot, but not a single person. I contemplated navigating the walk home in the hard darkness of night. It would take me hours to get to our apartment in the city. I was frozen with fear. How was I going to get home? How was I going to tell my mother I was fired?

I dropped down to the curb. I took off my sneakers, rubbing the baby toe on my right foot. It was sore from where a crumpled edge of the $20 bill had been poking into my flesh earlier. As the numbers on my digital watch passed one o'clock in the morning, the air grew colder. I hugged my knees to my chest, resting my forehead on my knees, shivering in my shorts and T-shirt.

"Are you okay?" a voice called out from the dark.

The security guard I had passed as I walked from the public area of the park to the employee side was standing in front of me, still in his uniform. I had no idea they worked this late and at the moment, I was grateful to have been found by another human being.

"I missed the last bus," I sniffled, "and I don't have another quarter to call my dad for a ride."

"Let's go into admin. You can use the phone at reception."

I followed him to the front door of the building. He pulled a key ring from his waist, attached to a belt loop on his pants. The tinkling of the keys was music to my ears. He led me to reception, then stood off to the side as I called my father.

When I told him I missed the last bus and my mom told me to call him, he sighed, heavily.

"I'll be there in about half an hour."

The security guard left me sitting on the bench outside the building. He wasn't allowed to let anybody in, he told me. I didn't argue. No sense in anyone else getting fired today.

"Strict rules on the night shift," he said, apologetically. He told me he would be inside, checking to make sure all was good and then he would have his lunch at the reception desk to make sure I was picked up.

I had 30 minutes to figure out how to explain what had happened. My mother, I knew, was going to flip out, but I had zero experience with how my father would handle this.

When my dad pulled up in his station wagon, I

glanced behind me. The security guard was standing just inside the doors of the building. I raised my hand to wave and he did the same.

"Hi Dane." My dad smiled at me as he rolled down the passenger window. We pulled out of the lot in silence. Not even the radio was playing.

As we pulled onto the highway, he couldn't take the quiet anymore.

"Lucky thing I wasn't asleep yet. How did you miss the bus?"

Without warning, the tears exploded from my eyes. I was sobbing. All the stress and fear and anxiety poured out. My dad reached behind me, passing me a box of tissues from the back seat. He didn't say a word as we drove south through the quiet streets north of Toronto.

"Care to share?" he asked after I blew my nose and wiped my face.

"I… I… was fired. For stealing." There was nothing more to it than that.

My dad was silent for a while. I looked down at my hands, wringing and shredding the wet tissues.

"Are they pressing charges?"

"I don't think so," I muttered. "They took my uniform and told me I was fired for stealing money."

"Did you?"

"Yeah."

"That was stupid."

"Yeah."

"You're lucky they aren't pressing charges. You got off easy this time."

"I know."

"How much did you steal? You know what? It doesn't matter. Will you do it again?"

I shook my head. "No." At that moment, I had no plans of ever stealing again. This was the second time I had been caught. Maybe thievery was not a good career choice for me.

"Lesson learned, then," my dad said, reaching over to give my shoulder a squeeze.

We were silent for the rest of the trip. When he pulled up in front of my apartment building and threw the gear into park, he turned to look directly at me.

"Good luck with your mother. What are you going tell her?"

I didn't know. I was terrified of telling her I was fired. I could already envision the disappointment on her face and the criticism in her voice. I hugged my dad, thanking him for coming to get me.

It was almost two o'clock in the morning. The lobby of the building was empty, the lights dimmed. When I got to our apartment door, my hand was shaking as I put the key in the lock. I opened the door, fully prepared to see the scorn and annoyance written on my mother's face. Instead, I was greeted with darkness. I felt a second of relief before I realized that my mother didn't care enough to wait up for me.

I spent the rest of the night tossing and turning in my bed, thoughts running through my head like a horse at a racetrack. What would I tell my mother? Would I ever be able to find another job? Why was I so stupid? Was stealing $20 or $40 here and there worth the risk? I was looking to line my pockets and thought I was making a friend. It was 100% a dumb thing to do.

I didn't tell my mother anything and she never asked.

But it's true what they say: You never forget your first.

———————————————

1. Names have been changed.

4

Taking Me to the Cleaners

D espite my worry I'd never get another job after being fired from Wonderland, I had plenty of jobs throughout the rest of high school. I went through jobs almost as often as I went through hair colours. I worked at a small local grocery store where I learned mice and bugs were an unavoidable part of the land-scape. I spent more than a year and a half working for an office supply retailer, where my love for pens was seeded (until I worked there, I had only known of three kinds of pens: Bic Stic pens, the BiWay discount store brand Bic knockoffs, and the Bic four-colour retractable click pen my single working mother couldn't afford to buy me). I spent one evening shift working for a tele-marketer before I walked out the door after being told off, sworn at, and hung up on after four attempted calls. I thought about claiming I had a family emergency until I realized that was probably not an original excuse to walk off that shit job. Instead, I called my supervisor over to the bank of phones I sat at and told him I didn't like this job and was leaving. I sailed out the door with a wave, marvelling at the people who chose to stay.

My next job was an hour-long bus ride away from my home, but an eight-minute walk from where my best friend/biggest crush lived. I deliberately sought a job in that neighbourhood, *because* it was so far from home and kept me away from the suffocating atmosphere there for longer. Also, I was 16 and thought I was in love.

On the days I was scheduled to work at the dry cleaners, Jake and I took the bus from school together. If there was time before my shift started, we hung out at his house, listening to music and having an after-school snack. This was my teenage heaven: laying on his futon, playing with the loose curls on his head, listening to Billy Bragg or Bob Marley.

I'd walk from his place to work, floating on clouds every step of the way. Once I was inside, though, the fog evaporated into the steam and stink of the dry cleaners. The smell was a sweet and sour combination of chemicals that repulsed me and made me hungry at the same time. I manned the front desk, grateful to not have to be in the back actually cleaning and pressing the clothes. I worked minimal hours when I started that spring. Most of my shift was taken up by customers picking up their dry cleaning, with very few dropping off. In the late 1980s, nothing was computerized, so all incoming clothes needed to be manually tagged and sorted. At first, I was grossed out by touching other people's dirty clothes to staple the number tags to button holes, belt loops, and waistbands. Regular customers had big blue numbered laundry bags they could just drop off. I nearly vomited the first time I reached into one of those bags and felt wetness under my fingers. From that point forward, I dumped the contents on the floor behind the counter so I could see what I was touching. For the most part, the clothes were just soiled in ordinary ways: wine, sweat, surface dirt, food stains, grease. Occasionally, there were other stains: blood, crotch juice, unidentifiable organic matter. My employers did not provide me with gloves and it never occurred to me to ask.

The actual dry cleaning happened in the back of the building. Without exception, every machine was operated by someone who wasn't a native English speaker. It was lonely at the front of the store, and I would drift to the back, chatting with Maria or Manny or Krystina or Dimitri or Svetlana. They came from places I had never been and was discouraged from ever visiting. It was the time of Corazon Aquino and military coups, Fidel Castro, and the KGB.

By the beginning of June, the heat in the shop was almost unbearable. When I took on more shifts throughout the summer, I propped open the front and back doors in the morning so a breeze could blow through, giving the team in the back a break. There was air conditioning in the front area of the store where the customers came in, but the plant in the back didn't have any. With the dry cleaning machines, the pressers, and the steamers going all day, it was a waste to try to cool the area.

Among my duties was running through the conveyor, checking invoice slips, and pulling out items hanging there for six months or more. It was a curiosity to me how people could forget to retrieve their clothes. I imagined such a luxury was only for the wealthy. In my house, losing a glove meant I would have a cold hand for at least two pay periods.

The job was not a glamorous one, but I had so much autonomy, which was a valuable gift for a teenager. The owners/bosses, Burt and Gabriella, were usually only in the plant early in the morning, gathering the previous day's receipts and collecting the money to take to the bank. They owned three franchise locations and divided their time among all of them. They had to trust that I would do my job well.

Jake occasionally came to hang out with me. He was there one day as I was running the conveyor and checking dates on all the slips. It was a hot day, and the air conditioning in the front was losing to the heat of the machines in the back. As my sweaty hands touched every slip to check the dates, they stuck to the plastic wrapping the clothing. I kept wiping my hands on my apron, but the sweat never evaporated. The ink from the thermal paper receipts transferred to my fingers. I wasn't paying attention to the wrapped items as I passed them to Jake, who made exclamations that were funny only because I was madly in love with him.

"This goes in the abandoned bride pile."

"I didn't know polyester suits were still around."

"A waist this small should only exist on a chihuahua."

"Nobody gets between me and my bejewelled Calvins."

I ran through the conveyor twice, making sure I didn't miss anything. When I was done, I had 46 phone calls to make.

Among the abandoned: a wedding dress, a Bob Mackie velvet gown, and the usual assortment of suits, skirts, and blouses. There was a man's suit with so many ruffles, I'd at first thought it was a dress; when I checked the label, the name was unfamiliar to me: Jean Paul Gaultier. Four years later, the name would become synonymous with Madonna's cone corset.

I made the phone calls, dialing numbers that were no longer in service, talking to people who had no idea who I was looking for, and leaving awkward messages on answering machines. By call #19, I had learned to tell the difference between a genuine "I forgot about it," those who had a painful memory attached to the item, and people who once had the money for luxury clothes, but now couldn't pay the dry cleaning fee.

But the most intriguing item, and the one that haunts me to this day: a police officer's uniform.

When I made the call, a woman answered.

"Hi, I'm calling from the dry cleaners. I have a uniform here for…" I took another look at the label, "McLean?"

I was met with silence on the other end.

"Hello? Are you still there?"

"You can get rid of that," the woman said.

"Like, throw it out? Why?" Dumb 16-year-old hasn't a clue.

A pause, then a tense answer. "He's dead. He died."

My face burned with discomfort. Without the experience of how to handle situations like this, I blurted out the first stupid thing that came to mind.

"Like, at work?"

A question I followed up with another ignorant gem.

"So, like, don't you want to keep this for, like, a memory?"

Understandably, the phone went dead in my hand.

When I told Jake, his eyes lit up.

"So, if they don't want it, can I have it?"

"What? Isn't it illegal to wear a police uniform if you're not, you know, a police officer?" I crinkled my brow and looked at him.

"Who knows. But it would be an amazing Halloween costume."

For longer than was appropriate, I considered letting him have it. Teen girl crushes make us stupid, but I wasn't wholly insensitive to how gross this would be. I struggled to come up with a way to tell him no that wouldn't sound like I was disapproving. I wanted him to love me, not think I was uncool. I could have said Gabriella asked me to track and report and I would get in trouble, especially if she knew this uniform was here. I could have told him to wait a few more weeks to see if someone came to get it.

"No," I told him firmly. "That is not cool, Jake."

He shrugged, then gave me that killer lopsided smile that made my whole body tingle.

"Okay. I've got to go. See you tomorrow."

He sauntered out of the store, his curls kissing the back of his sweaty neck. That was the day I started loving him less.

5

Rich and Famous and Chronically Late

One of my childhood friends had the most awesome mother. A Brit with a fantastic accent, Liv's makeup reminded me of a character from *Coronation Street*. Her eyes were always heavily coloured with a bright selection from her rainbow palette, her false lashes always painted thick with black mascara. She was a huge personality and everything she did was exaggerated. She was unapologetically exuberant, and, as a single mom, defiantly proud of her accomplishments.

Liv was a natural-born storyteller. The stories she told her daughters and me about her work in a couture fashion shop left us scandalized. For the entirety of her adult life, Liv worked for a women's fashion designer, one of the most prominent ones in Toronto from the 1980s through to the early 2000s. Her clientele included the most famous and wealthiest not only in Toronto, but from around the world. If they made headlines, they were on Liv's client list.

Without revealing anyone's identity, Liv regaled us with stories of women who *had* to have leather in every piece they wore, women who refused to buy anything others in their circle may have bought, women who stopped wearing underwear, and women who insisted they were a size four when they were really a size six or larger.

"When this woman tried something on, I lied to her, telling her we put a size six label on everything in the store," Liv told us. "Our seamstresses in the back would switch out the size labels before they bagged the clothing for delivery. It was important that we all perpetuate the illusion."

Another time, while Liv was preparing dinner for us from dented cans of soup, she told us about a client who insisted pizza be ordered every time she visited the store, which was by appointment only.

"Daft cow owned a chain of fitness studios and could *never* order pizza at home. Told us she did it to see how the clothes would look if she was bloated. We weren't bloody idiots. We all knew she was hiding her indulgences. It was me who had to convince her to wear cloth gloves when she tried things on so the grease from her fingers wouldn't bugger up the clothing. We neglected to notice the drippings on her lips. Bunch of jiggery-pokery, that was."

The idiosyncrasies of these shoppers were engaging and endless. We'd laugh until we were crying. As the children of single working moms, this was the only exposure we had to the ridiculously wealthy. My adolescent brain took comfort in stories about how being rich didn't mean you were immune from being a weirdo.

Liv had clients who were kind and generous, but she also had those who treated her like garbage.

"I've seen them all, girls," she let us know with a smile pasted on her face. "In one shift, I've had ladies ask me for suggestions about what would look good on them and others who would tell me I was just there to bring things out and keep my mouth shut. I've been called stupid, lazy, and useless, but I've also been told I'm funny, kind, and patient. It's all true."

"Mom, you can't be all those things at the same time," my friend protested.

"To the customer, I can. I'm whatever they decide I am. They can say whatever they want when I'm inside the shop. I don't need their approval. They are not my friends. I know who I am and I'm proud of that. A woman buying a gown will never change that."

"Aren't you ever intimidated by these women?" I asked.

Liv laughed and shook her head.

"You know what, Dana? They are just people whose jobs are different from mine."

Liv's lessons came to mind when I started working at a video rental store in a posh Toronto neighbourhood. These were the same people Liv had worked for her entire career. When I found myself slipping into awe, or falsely believing that I was part of their world, Liv's voice pulled me back into reality.

Their job is just different. They are just people. They are not my friends.

I was there to serve, to make recommendations, to get to know the kind of movies they liked. I paid attention to the details you only notice when someone is a frequent customer. I knew when the bank executive's kids had left for summer camp because he and his wife would stop renting children's movies for two months. When the model started renting action films with lots of gratuitous violence, I knew, before the media did, that she had been through another breakup. Not all our customers were rich and famous, but everyone filled the small paper bags with free popcorn and left a buttery trail of bits throughout the store. Free is free, no matter your financial status.

Like other video rental stores, we charged late fees. Most people came in with their late movies wearing a sheepish look. Some asked for forgiveness, but others demanded it. Those who could afford to pay tenfold were usually the ones making the biggest fuss over a $2 late fee. The rudeness varied:

"Do you have any idea who I am? How dare you."

"I could buy this whole store and never pay a late fee again."

"You don't make the decisions here. I do."

"Is this how you get a power trip in your sad little life?"

I heard Liv in my head again. *Money can buy you nice things, but it will never buy you class. Just smile and be the stupid person they have already decided you are.*

I did exactly that. Sometimes I would shrug my shoulders, indicating that I was helpless in this situation and they could talk to Mick, the owner. If they refused to pay, I left the balance outstanding on their account. I knew Mick ran a monthly report and made phone calls, chasing down the late fees.

One day, a regular customer came in with two plastic bags full of videos. I knew this family well. *Everyone* in Toronto knew the members of this iconic entertainment family.

"These are very late," he said, hefting the bags onto the counter. "And we are very sorry."

I smiled and started scanning the videos back into the system. He had almost two dozen videotapes in the bags, all children's videos. I knew he had three young kids.

"Oh my…" fell out of my mouth when I glanced at the total late charges.

He sighed as he pulled out his wallet.

"I know, I know. They are ridiculously late. We went to Japan for three weeks and just forgot about them. What do I owe?"

"More than it would cost to just buy the videos yourself. Maybe you should just buy stuff from now on. It would be cheaper." I smiled, unsure how he would take my advice.

"No, thanks. It's bad enough the kids watch them repeatedly for the week we have them. I don't want this stuff in my house permanently. I'll lose my mind."

As he handed over his credit card, I wanted to offer to waive the fees. He was *so nice*. All the time. His wife was lovely, too. The children, on the odd occasion all three were in the store, were polite, rarely squabbling over which videos to pick.

"I can offer you a discount on the late fees. Fifty percent. That takes it down to just over $100."

"No, really. I don't mind paying the fees. Please charge the full price. If my wife finds out I got a discount, I'll be in trouble."

I laughed, then rang through the full charges. *Classy is not asking for special treatment and paying the price like everyone else.*

You'd think it would be dull working in a video store, but that was not my experience. As a clerk, I was privy to conversations I wasn't meant to overhear and life stories of people who were way outside my social sphere. This was especially true of our regular customers who came to trust my recommendations and thus, came to trust me with some of their darkest secrets. It's a lot to process when an extremely famous television personality tells you that at least once per week, they consider screaming "Fuck you all" live on the program they host and walking off the set to live in a hut in Thailand.

Other perks included access to new releases before anyone else and an endless supply of popcorn. Less of a perk was having to use the hole in the floor behind the service desk to peep into the adult section in the basement. I thought it was to ensure no children went in there, but Mick informed me it was to make sure no one was having sex before checking out *Jurassic Pork* or *The Madam's Family*. While I was lucky to never have to put a stop to half-naked activity, I did once have to make an uncomfortable phone call regarding some fully naked activity.

Only once during the two years I worked there did a homemade porn movie get left in a rented camera. Did I watch it? Not only did I watch it, I called my friend Kevin, who lived above the store, to tell him about it.

"I'll be there in five minutes. Make some fresh popcorn."

Kevin, who was flamboyantly gay, could not get over how someone would forget to take *that* tape out of the camera.

"Do you think they'll come back for it?" he asked.

"I don't know, but I'm supposed to call the customer when this happens."

"Oh my gawd! I would die if it was me getting that call."

"Would you come collect the tape? Or would you be too embarrassed?"

"Honey. Look at me. Look at this body." Kevin was a health nut, cut perfectly, with angles everywhere. Adorable face, killer bod. "*Of course*, I'd collect my tape. I'm proud of my work, but I don't want to share it with the world."

We watched for less than five minutes.

"So boring," Kevin said. He kissed the air next to my face and went home.

I made the call, relieved to leave a message rather than talk to one of the stars of the movie. A man in his early 20s came in the next day to retrieve the tape. He blushed and avoided eye contact. When he was gone, I called Kevin, reporting that the tape was picked up.

"You know what?" I laughed. "The camera really does add 15 pounds."

6

The 50-Million-Dollar Woman

When I graduated—for the second time—from university, I held two degrees, possessed zero practical skills, and owed the bank a lot of money for my student loans. After unsuccessfully trying to land a full-time job in journalism, I found a job working part-time at a horse racetrack, taking bets and paying out winnings. I was there for almost a year when I stumbled upon an ad in a newspaper for a hiring fair for the as-yet-to-be-opened Casino Niagara. I was intrigued for two reasons: one, the opportunity to be gainfully employed, and two, to have an address that was almost 150 kilometres away from my overbearing mother.

I drove to Niagara Falls, resumé and writing samples in hand, to apply for any kind of job. Given my educational background in journalism, I was hoping for a job in communications or public relations. I envisioned myself cranking out internal newsletters, feeding press releases to the media, and being part of the marketing team. Given my actual work experience, I was expecting to land a job as a cashier.

After my initial screening interview, I was moved on to the next round. The two interviewers looked over my resumé. I was asked about my work as a key holder at the video store. We chatted about my years at the bank. They were curious about what I had done at the racetrack and they seemed elated to discover I already had experience in the gaming industry, meaning I was one step ahead with the required police checks. They asked why I wanted to work at the casino.

"I like the pace in gaming. There's always something interesting happening," I answered.

"What do you see yourself doing there?"

"I'd love to work in communications or marketing," I said. One recruiter looked down at my resumé, while the other got this weird look that I would later come to identify as the "wants a job they are not qualified for" look. I myself would develop a talent for that look when I became a hiring manager: slight head tilt, lips pressed thin, eyes scanning the room for the next candidate.

"But I'd be happy just to start anywhere," I quickly added, sensing the interview was starting to crumble.

When both of the women sitting on the other side of the folding table smiled at me, I knew that was the right answer.

For the entire hour and a half drive home, I imagined myself moving out and finally living life on my own terms. Having already spent a summer as a reporter in St. Catharines, I was familiar with the

Niagara peninsula. I was excited about trying to find an apartment, buying some furniture, and living without my mother's scrutiny.

By the time I got home from the job fair, there was a message on my answering machine offering me a job as a foreign exchange cashier. I had no idea what that was. It didn't matter. My life was finally about to begin.

For two weeks, I commuted from Toronto to Niagara Falls for my training. We were in a decommissioned school, an old brick building tucked away in a corner of the city where there were no homes or industry. It was a weird place for a school. The main office was boarded up from the inside, and a length of chain with a padlock the size of a football sealed off the gym. The horror movie/zombie apocalypse vibe was broken by the chatter drifting out of the classrooms. Almost every room on both floors was being used by the various departments in the casino: table games, food and beverage, customer service, back of house, and bank, where I would be working.

Day one was all about getting to know my colleagues. The energy was high in the classroom. The casino was still under construction and being part of the opening team was exciting. There were 30 of us in that room, sitting at worn down, scratched, and etched wood-topped desks with matching chairs. I ran my fingers over the "Fuck You, Mr. B" scraped in the upper left corner of my desk and grinned. I was happy to no longer be in high school, steeped in the angst and hormones of teen life.

After introductions, we were grouped in fours. We

pushed the front of our desks together, forming a square—me, Lucy, Monica, and another young woman whose name I've since forgotten. She would not last the week, vanishing from class before Friday, along with six others. It perplexed me because the training was easy. Basic math, balancing our play money, finding errors. We were never told how to fix problems or what the protocol was for figuring out where you made a mistake. I drew on my experience at the bank, where the paper trail was the first place you looked for an error. I didn't know it yet, but this was the job that was going to reveal my forensic accounting skills.

I had no idea the training was not only assessing our skills, but testing our ability to handle stress. We role-played guest scenarios. We were given complicated transactions. We sometimes had to read minds and figure out what the guest was really asking for and manage difficult behaviours. Our recruiters were deciding who had the mettle to be on the most chal-lenging shift in a casino: the swing shift.

The swing shift ran from 3 p.m. to 1 a.m., with start times at 3, 4, or 5 p.m. In every casino around the world, the swing shift is the hardest, fastest, and most fascinating to work. The pace is hectic, the demands are great. Most days, it was non-stop service. Handling the rush, the high rollers, and the after-dinner crowd made us the casino elite.

Once it was safe to do so, we were allowed inside the mostly finished casino building, getting to know our workspace before it was opened to the public. For a week before opening, all hands were called to work, to either practise our jobs or act as guests. I played baccarat for the first time in the high rollers' section (something that would never happen in real life). I won a massive (fake) jackpot at the dollar slots. I ate in Farfalle, the five-star restaurant inside the casino. I tried to stay serious as I dealt with a cute fellow employee playing an angry man who had lost everything and was taking it out on me. I was grateful for the heavy, bullet-proof glass separating me from the spittle of my fake customer (I would see him again, later, in the loss prevention department when I suspected a man of trying to cash fake traveller's cheques. I won employee of the month for catching that guy, who was passing off counterfeits all over the Niagara peninsula. Now that I'm much, much older, I feel the reward for stopping a man who had already cashed more than $10,000 in fakes should have been better than a paper certificate and dinner at Farfalle with the other employees of the month).

For eight hours a day at one of two sets of foreign exchange windows, seven of my colleagues and I changed American dollars into Canadian dollars and back again. We cashed traveller's cheques from all over the world. We gave directions, cashed chips, and were some of the first people guests saw when they came into the building (aside from valet and gift shop staff).

Over the course of my two years, I saw the best and the worst of humankind. I learned two things bring people to a casino: the dream of winning lots of money or a plan for a night out where they drop a hundred bucks including drinks, dinner, and some pulls on the arm of the nickel slots.

The brides-to-be, the last-night-bachelors, and the 18-year-olds who crossed the border to drink made up the bulk of people looking for a fun night out. More than once, I had to answer these questions from Americans who crossed the 49th parallel for the first time:

- How does this whole casino thing work?
- Can I use real money here?
- What time do the Falls turn off?
- When does winter start in Canada?

At the start, I would politely answer—or try to answer—their questions:

- It's best if you just walk in and have look around, then decide what you want to play. Like you're assessing a buffet.
- American dollars are not accepted inside the casino. I'll change it for Canadian dollars.
- You mean the lights? They turn off at midnight, but the Falls run all the time.
- Same date as in America. December 21.

Over time, though, our answers became as ludicrous as the questions:

- How does this whole casino thing work? You empty your wallet and leave with way less money than you came in with. Coat check is also card check. You can leave your credit and debit cards with them to prevent overspending. (Coat check, who were fun people too, enjoyed ping-ponging the guests back to us seeking the free Susan B. Anthony collectable coin we were supposed to give them.)

- Can I use real money here? No, sadly. The Canadian government was bought by Parker Brothers and we are mandated to use Monopoly money throughout the country.
- What time do the Falls turn off? Hard to say. We never know when they will run out of water.
- When does winter start? Oh, it can blow in here at any moment. Did you bring a parka and snowshoes with you just in case?

You'd think we would have been reprimanded for our snarky behaviour, but the gaming industry isn't like a normal retailer. One supervisor had a Ziploc bag (it had to be a clear bag, because loss prevention always had to know we weren't concealing anything) filled with fun-size candy bars and Werther's caramel candies. She would reward us for balancing to the penny, helping a co-worker, staying on shift for an extra hour or two when someone called in sick, and for the smarmiest answer of the shift. In year two, the best answer was rewarded with a full-size candy bar. She did what she could to balance the gruelling pace, the nasty behaviour, and the general air of depression that permeates the casino. (For you empaths, the next time you are in one, take note: that heavy feeling of confusion and overwhelm is the emotional grab bag of winning and losing.)

Part of my job was issuing cash advances on credit cards. If you've never used your credit card for a cash advance, you're lucky. It's a measure of last resort, a means to borrow money from the only source left. Borrowing money against your credit card is the first step into real, debilitating debt. The minute I approve the advance, you start paying the full rate of interest (often 20% or more), not only on the cash you take out, but on every purchase you make with that card after that date.

At the casino, requesting a credit card advance required the patron to present identification along with their card. More than once, as I handed over a pile of cash, I tried to ignore the photos of little kids I saw when the wallet was opened. I would think about those kids when the patron came back for more money again and again. With every swipe of the card, until the limit was maxed out, I'd be thinking about what daddy would tell them when they asked for a new bike or a doll.

Sister Mary Elizabeth is the one guest I'll carry in my mind forever. When she first came to my window seeking a cash advance, she was just like any other guest. She wore cotton elasticized beige pants and a simple buttoned blouse. She had glasses and a lovely, friendly smile that reached the corners of her eyes. When she handed me her credit card, my brain thought maybe her first name really was Sister. When she pulled out her driver's licence, I was stunned to see her identified as a nun.

My colleagues and I discussed this at length. As a Jew, I had no idea how Catholicism worked. My best friend, a non-practicing Catholic, was perplexed about how a nun could even get a credit card.

"They don't even have an income," one co-worker said.

"How can she even make payments?" wondered another.

"Maybe she left the sisterhood," someone else said.

Once a month, Sister Mary Elizabeth would show up at my window, credit card at the ready. I once joked with her that maybe she should try a different cashier. Gamblers are a superstitious lot, and they attach their beliefs to winning as much as losing.

"I have faith," she said. "God is telling me to come to you and I believe him."

I wasn't going to argue. I wasn't a big believer in God, but I also knew the #1 rule of gaming: the house always has the advantage. Compulsive gamblers will never, ever come out ahead. They will win and lose over and over until they have nothing left.

Sister Mary Elizabeth must have had someone watching over her though. She did come to my window with winnings once after two years. She won over $10,000 at a slot machine. She was smiling from ear to ear as I changed her Canadian dollars back to American. She didn't seem bothered that she was only taking away a little more than $7,000 US.

She took a $100 bill from her stack and passed it back to me through the window. A tip for my service, the largest I had ever received.

"Thank you for being nice all the time," she said. "I may be back one day, but now God is telling me to stop and I always listen." She put the money into her purse and walked away from the window, waving her hand above her head. I never saw the sister again.

Eventually, I was moved from the windows to the caged bank where I counted money all day—$8 million in cash that had to balance to the penny. It wasn't as amusing as being at the window, but managing the flow of money in and out every day was the break I needed to reset myself and my emotions. Dealing face-to-face with gamblers—especially compulsive ones—was draining and heartbreaking. It was also my first-ever promotion. Not only did I take on more responsibility and earn more per hour, I felt I had earned it through hard work and a developing skill set. It was a merit-based promotion, such that I would never see again for the rest of my working life.

For the next year, I was focused on managing the money and not gamblers. I was pulled to other areas of the casino, having built a reputation as a wizard at finding errors. Once, I was sent to the main bank, where a $5 shortage was proving elusive. I started at the beginning, spending the next three and a half hours meticulously counting more than $50 million in cash and chips, checking the paperwork of every cashier. I followed the paper trail and found nothing.

Perplexed, I pulled all the drawers out as far as they

would go, preparing to start all over again. As I pulled one drawer, I heard a sound that didn't fit. I peered inside, then squeezed my hand into the narrow spaces between the stacks of wrapped bills and the edges of the drawer. My fingernails scraped something at the back. I pulled out the money, bundles of $100 bills, $10,000 at a time, until I could see the back edge. There, buried in the darkness and the smell of fresh ink from the bills, was a $5 chip. It was wedged at the back, sitting on its edge in the darkness. I was thanked for my efforts and sent back to my own cage. I wasn't at the casino much longer after that. I thought my skills would be rewarded again and I would be promoted, but that never happened. After two and a half years on the swing shift, I was burnt out. I needed a break, a job with less pressure where I could carry a purse that wasn't transparent.

And I found it in a job that would swing my career into the depths of retail. I took a 50% pay cut to go work at a large-format bookstore, where I learned both what it meant to be a manager and how to cope with devastating heartbreak.

7

Meeting a Unicorn

I t's rare to find a lifer in retail. Turnover is normal
and expected at the employee and management
levels. General managers (also known as store
managers) shuffle more than pieces on a chess board.
They generally last in a store for three to five years
before they are moved either to another store or into a
higher level position such as regional manager. RMs
burn out in five to eight years because districts and
regions can be huge. One manager I know covers a
region from Manitoba to Vancouver Island and north to
Yellowknife. One person to cover more than half of the
country, geographically. Retail, at any level, is not for
the faint of heart.

When you find someone in a retail store who has
been there for more than 10 years, you need to acknowledge that you've met a freaking unicorn.

Those who choose the retail life are easy to spot.
Lifers are a sure sign that a company is good to work
for. I know this firsthand. As a manager, I learned

turnover was higher when the company overall—or the general manager—was shit. No matter how strong my working relationship was with my staff, no matter how deep the discounts or how flexible the schedule, a garbage corporation will have a hard time keeping good people. So when someone says they've been with a company for more than five years, that says more about the business than the person.

Lifers come in with a smile every single day. They vibrate with energy when they turn a confused customer into a happy one. After a period of time working a sales floor, their ears become attuned to the needs of customers, like a mother who senses her babies will cry before she hears the first murmur. I myself honed this skill while I was doing time. I developed the ability to discern between the people who are clearly lost in the store, the shoppers who have a specific mission, and the browsers who have zero intention of spending a dime. I felt the nuances of a kind person, sensed the energy of the problem customers, and recognized the panic of someone not being able to find what they needed RIGHT NOW. I built the skill of unintentionally eavesdropping, subconsciously listening for ways to help.

Lifers make great managers because they invest time in their employees and can be found on the sales floor. A manager who hides in the office, avoiding interactions with customers and employees on the sales floor, will be moving on as soon as something better comes along.

Jennifer, the first retail store manager I worked for,

was one of those people whose part-time retail job evolved into a managerial role. After graduating high school, she found her place in the retail world. She had the right personality: patience, a desire to learn, the ability to teach, and a high tolerance for bullshit. Jennifer was 100% a smile and nod and make it work kind of person. Her ambition was to one day be the general manager for a store, and she got there within two years. She was already more than a decade into her career when she hired me, but at the time, I had no idea she was a unicorn in this business.

The newly built Chapters bookstore was a shell when I walked in on my first day. Gondolas—the double-sided merchandise display units—had been placed, and shelves had been built into the walls. I could still smell the paint.

Before we opened the store to the public, Jennifer was in the weeds with all of us. She moved fixtures, hauled boxes of books around the store, and washed windows. She broke her nails and had dirt on her face like the rest of us. She trained employees, starting with the first lesson of "customer service begins in the parking lot." She encouraged us to leave the best parking spots for the people who were coming to the store to spend their money.

Once we were opened, Jennifer spent most of her time on the sales floor. I watched how she engaged with customers. I soaked up every piece of advice she gave me that could make me better at my job. I realized she set her team up for success, and it showed in her employee retention rates. We had very little turnover at our store.

I had been hired as the front-end lead, supervising and scheduling the cashiers, balancing and logging the sales numbers, managing the cash, and merchandising the bargain books section as well as the impulse buys displayed at the register. Special orders also fell under my miscellaneous duties and responsibilities. It was an entry-level management position and I walked the floor with my head held high. I had *responsibilities.* I made *decisions.* I was *in charge.* Unlike the casino, the book-store held more promise of moving into a corporate position. At our orientation, we were told about all the opportunities for advancement, both within the store and the company. It was heady stuff for someone in her late 20s.

A true test came for me when there was a company-wide management restructuring, less than a year after I started. On the day head office sent out our new titles, I was demoted to senior bookseller. Gone was the sched-uling for the cashiers. The codes on the cash office door and the combination to the safe were changed. Within 15 minutes of me starting my day, I had been down-graded from manager to minion.

My cashiers gave me pitying looks. I was lost for what to do with my day. The change blindsided me, the rug swept out from under me. I had left a lucrative job to be there. I was stinging from the bruised ego, from feeling left out, from being cut off from the inner circle of management. I was treated like a child whose parents were punishing her and taking away all her favourite toys. I deserved better than this.

In the bathroom, I cried for at least a half hour. When I emerged, I wandered back to the front of the store, uncertain what to do. I stepped behind the counter, stood at a cash register, and blankly stared out into the centre of the store. I smiled thinly at the customers. I could not even look at my fellow cashiers. Nancy, a full-time cashier who yesterday was my direct report, stood beside me, then told me she was sorry to hear the news. My eyes filled with tears again and I drifted back to the bathroom.

"Dana, are you okay?" Jennifer had come looking for me.

I held my breath, wishing she would leave.

"Listen," she said, "I know this is crappy and I understand why you're upset. There's a reason this happened, but I can't tell you much more than that."

My tears were slowing and I was entering the next stage of grief: anger.

I wiped my face and pulled open the door of the stall, ready to tear a strip off her. I breathed through my nose, trying to calm myself. Yelling at my boss would not be useful.

"Of course I'm upset. I've worked so hard to get where I am. Am I not doing my job well? I've moved from being in charge to having zero responsibility. Do you know how embarrassing it is to be at the same level as the people you once managed?"

"I get it, I do. It's not easy for me to deliver the news. You have been doing a great job and, yeah, it's shitty what happened. Can you just trust me that it's for the better?"

I couldn't see how being demoted was a good thing. I didn't want to go back to the sales floor with my new job and my tear-smeared face.

"Can I take the rest of the day off? I need to go home and process this."

"Sure." Jennifer nodded. "I think it takes a very mature person to recognize when she needs to step away from something."

In my apartment, I wallowed. This was my first taste of career loss in my adult life. I ate two large bags of chips. I booted up my super slow computer and began a search for a new job. I cried some more. I called my boyfriend, who let me rant and make empty threats about telling them to go to hell as I quit. By that evening, I had walked through all the emotions. My innate desire to keep fighting kicked in. I was not going to let this blip derail my career. Jennifer told me to trust her and I was going to do exactly that.

The next day, I went to work, ready to take on the new challenge. After my day at home, I realized I had lost a title and some face, but my pay was the same. My passion for books was the same. The people I enjoyed working with were still there. I had nothing to pout about, really. I had accepted that this was my new reality and I was powerless to change it. The only thing I could control was how I managed myself going forward. I continued to do my job well, acting like a mid-level supervisor. My days were easier without the pressures of scheduling and money management. I taught other full-timers how to merchandise smartly. I looked for ways to make the front cash run more efficiently. I moved the special orders from a desk at the far side of the store to the front where we had quick access and customers didn't have to wait at an empty desk for someone to notice them.

One month after my demotion, I was offered a newly created position—zone manager—at a new store in another city. This was the opportunity I was waiting for: the chance to be in the direct sightlines of head office and to start my climb up the ladder. The whole "restructuring" had been an exercise to weed out the petty from the ambitious. At the time, my ambition blinded me. It never once occurred to me that toying with emotions and playing these kinds of games was demoralizing. Many managers who were also demoted to senior booksellers or leads left the company. There were tales of angry managers refusing to take one step outside the job descriptions in their new contracts, even if the requests fell under the "miscellaneous tasks" category. Those who held their heads high and aimed to do the best job they could were the keepers.

I was moved from St. Catharines to Toronto, to a two-storey store under construction that was to be a flagship for the company. I thrived. I made mistakes. I learned something new every day. When the books started coming in before our elevator and escalator were inspected and licensed, I hauled boxes up the stairs with all the employees. I was hot and dirty and sweaty every day. I was exhausted by the end of my shift. My nose was plugged with construction dust. It sounds awful, but opening a new store from the ground up is very exciting with a clear reward at the end: a shiny new store that has your fingerprints in every corner. On the first day of new employee orientation, I stood in front of a room of eager young people and said, "Customer service begins in the parking lot."

At the time, I couldn't imagine myself working anywhere else, but I also didn't see myself as a lifer on the sales floor. I set my sights on one day working at head office, maybe in planning for merchandising or as a buyer or maybe even a district manager. The best way to move to head office, I thought, was to do my job well, hire and train great employees, and not be afraid to take chances. I would eventually learn that in retail, doing the right thing isn't necessarily rewarded.

8

Rah, Rah, Go Rah Yourself

The first morning meeting of my career was with Chapters and it was inspirational. The staff collected on the raised level, in front of the bestseller wall. The greats of fiction were watching over us: Stephen King, Dan Brown, Patricia Cornwell, and John Grisham. The non-fiction gurus were there too: Bill Bryson, Nigella Lawson, Simon Winchester, and Cokie Roberts.

After five weeks of hard labour, the bookstore was ready to open to the public. I was excited to be part of the opening team. I was ready to greet the customers, help them find what they sought, and make recommendations of my own favourites. We stood in random form, not quite a circle, waiting for Jennifer, our general manager. I held a coffee in my hand, savouring the last few sips.

"Okay, team," Jennifer said as she climbed the three steps to where we stood. "First, I want to thank you all for every second of hard work you put in getting this store ready." She paused, smiling at all of us. The spotlights caught her nose ring; the tiny diamond sparkled.

"It's our first day and I want you to remember some very important things. One, it's okay to tell a customer you don't know, but find someone who does. Two, if you see books lying around on tables and chairs, please put them away. Even if it's not your section. One day, it might be. Learn the store. Three, have fun and have a remarkable day."

"Woo-hoo!" I yelled, then tried to retreat. I worried maybe this wasn't appropriate morning meeting etiquette. Jennifer laughed, and the team started clapping.

Every morning meeting with Jennifer was filled with energy, even a year after we first opened the doors. Jennifer let us know when someone was celebrating a birthday or any other life milestone. We gathered in different parts of the store and she passed the torch to the manager of each section. She let us determine what we wanted to talk about at the morning meeting. I once spent 10 minutes talking about the puzzle books in the bargain books section. We had hundreds of volumes of Sudoku, crosswords, and word searches for all ages. Summer was coming, I pointed out to the team.

"These books are perfect for taking to the cottage or throwing into the car for road trips or gifting to someone who has an RV. Price points are between $5 and $15."

"We should put one in the lunchroom," one associate suggested.

Jennifer liked that idea, so she bought a mega book

of mixed puzzles and left it in the staff room. For the better part of a year, we all opened that book, some of us starting new puzzles while others finished off those already started. We collaborated without knowing who was involved.

It was brilliant of Jennifer to encourage each of the managers to take ownership of their sections and share information at the morning meetings. It helped us understand the challenges of each section. The morning meeting was an opportunity for professional growth: we could work on our presentation skills, try new ways to motivate the team, and get everyone invested in the success of the store. When Ruth, our children's books manager, took the "stage," I learned the section was in a constant state of disarray because little hands would pick up books, walk around, and then drop them whenever something new grabbed their attention. Melinda, who ran the self-help section, told us about some new books that had a lot of buzz: *Who Moved My Cheese?*, *The Four Agreements*, and *Life Strategies* by Dr. Phil, who at the time was rising to fame on *The Oprah Winfrey Show*.

Gradually, we handed the morning meetings over to the employees, inviting them to share what they were reading. It was great training for future managers. They had to learn how to present to a group in a short time, giving the most pertinent information while staying engaging. Michael forced his way out of his shell to tell us how he literally had white knuckles while reading *Into Thin Air*. Lisa couldn't stop gushing about *Angela's Ashes*. Nancy was in love with *Memoirs of a Geisha*.

The morning meetings were so enjoyable, it never

occurred to me until I was with another company that Jennifer's method was not the norm. She *never* talked about the sales numbers. She never demanded we push product on the customers. She was 100% invested in the people-first approach to both associates and customers. It was a rewarding foundation for me before I moved through the retail world, bringing this energy and flow to my own morning meetings.

But your morning meetings can only be as good as the manager allows. There was the general manager who spent the 15 minutes droning on about driving sales numbers. He bored us to tears, and really, the staff didn't care that men's denim was underperforming compared to last year. At another company, the store manager allowed the section managers to run the meetings, but only following her agenda. I once tried to sneak in some news about some of the crazy contraptions that debuted at the International Housewares Show in Chicago, but just as I was about to share the latest innovation in blenders—the Magic Bullet—I was cut off and the staff told to disperse to their sections.

Of all the meetings I've been party to, the ones that irk me the most are those that force a huddle. After we've been bored to tears about company performance, and not permitted to participate with our own input, it's tough to find the inspiration to lean close, pile your hand in a group, and raise your arms at the same time with an enthusiastic "Go Team!" It's fake and always left a bad taste in my mouth. In my head, the word "team" was replaced with "eff yourself!"

I can buy into the whole "rah, rah" mentality when I

am truly made to feel as if I'm a valuable member of the team. Most managers, sadly, don't acknowledge that their captive audience is only there for a paycheque. If you want your employees to be fully invested in the success of the store, you have to be fully invested in the success of the person. Jennifer understood that in order to motivate people you have to let them shine.

9

Dreaming Big and Budgeting Small

Working in the gaming industry pays well, but retail does not. When I applied for the management position at Chapters, I was in a position to absorb the substantial difference in my biweekly paycheques. The casino work had enabled me to pay off six years' worth of student loans in two years, pay all my other bills, and put some money away for the future. Cutting my pay in half meant I would have to budget well and make some small sacrifices en route to bigger things. It was a trade-off I was willing to make in pursuit of my new goal of getting off the sales floor and working my way into head office.

The salaries in retail management are never going to make you rich. The expectations and the hours far surpass the compensation. At any given time, I was barely making enough to cover all my expenses. My first apartment cost me less than $500 per month and what kept me afloat when I moved into retail was the pile of money I'd saved when I worked at the casino.

At the time of writing (late 2021), an internet search shows me salaries have not much improved since my first gig in 1998. The salary range for store management is $40,000 to $70,000 per year. If you land in the middle at $50,000, your pay, before deductions, is around $3,800 per month. On a 40-hour work week, you're earning $24 per hour, but let's be honest, no retail manager clocks less than 50 hours per week. And that's okay, because the demands of a salaried management position are going to suck any hope of work-life balance out of your soul anyway.

In very few cases, working in retail management can sustain all the basic necessities of life. Over the course of a decade, I made many sacrifices. I went for months without eating meat, getting my protein from the processed cheese I threw on top of my bowl of pasta. I made a can of tuna last for three sandwiches. I rarely went out, but I wasn't missing much since most of my friends were also retail managers. We worked wonky hours for little pay and did most of our socializing on the sales floor.

Here's something else to chew on: if management pay is so dismal, consider the wages of the hourly workers. Retail does not attract stellar candidates. It's a great job for students looking for part-time work or people who want to fill some time but don't really need the money to actually live on and pay bills. Most full-timers or managers have their eye on something else. Some bigger goal. Almost everyone in management had a university degree. Okay, so they were in impractical fields like philosophy, economics, or film studies (me!), which meant we were well-educated and well aware of how poorly we were being paid. We told ourselves it was temporary, that we'd find something else more in line with our university education. One of my full-time employees at the bookstore had three degrees and still no clue about what he wanted to do when he grew up. A fellow manager graduated at the top of her class with an honours bachelor of arts and after three years in retail, went back to school to study graphic design. I myself, after two university degrees and a truncated attempt at a master's degree in French, went back to school in the evenings to study marketing. Everyone in retail has a dream of being somewhere else.

Almost daily, I considered making a career change. But where would I go? With few tangible or marketable skills, I had very few choices. I couldn't circle back to journalism; I had been out of the business for too long and recent journalism school graduates were getting the few available jobs. I was trapped in the only industry that would have me. I convinced myself that I was destined for greater things, such as a role in a corporate environment. My barren bank account was a temporary thing. I planned to find my way off the sales floor.

I dove head-first in to learning everything I could about retail. From my very first week at Chapters, I was bombarded with a new vocabulary I had to memorize and throw around, demonstrating that I understood every word was underpinned by a connection to profit. For example:

Impulse Buys at POS: The items that attract the eye at the Point of Sale (the cash register) and typically have a high margin. It's the home for high-end chocolate bars and candy at the checkout. They typically carry a 30–50% markup. Also, ironically, home to the pieces of shit you'll use once, then exile to the junk drawer.

Fast Movers: These are the hot sellers, the inventory that has a fast sell-through rate. These will be featured in the centre of the store so customers have to pass a lot of other merchandise to get them, like passing through the casino floor to get to the hotel room elevators. I've watched more customers zip by, blind to the fast movers on their way to where they really want to go: the clearance at the back.

Traffic: Every store has counters at the entrances. If one entry point is busier than another, higher margin goods should be there. That's why cosmetics greet you as soon as you walk in any mall entrance in a department store, or why you pass through cosmetics as you go to buy cough medicine at the drugstore. With a 60% markup on the items, retailers want you to buy another concealer or lipstick. And if your feminism is triggered, you should know men's razors and blades fall into that same profit margin.

Average Customer Spend: The goal is to make customers spend more. Upsizing, deals of the week at the cash, and on-the-floor suggestions are ways to bring those dollars in. Even grocery stores are on the bandwagon, building "Make this for dinner tonight!" displays featuring all the ingredients needed to make said meal. I sold a lot of socks with a simple question: "How about some fun socks to go with that? Buy two pairs, get one free."

While encouraging a customer to spend an additional $6 might not seem like a big deal, it's important to note that retail is all about the bottom line. Every dollar counts. Investors—as in shareholders—were always watching our numbers, particularly our payroll percentages. In one management meeting, the team was told that 15% of our gross sales could be spent on payroll. Influencing 10 people to buy socks equated to another employee hour on the sales floor. However, on paper and in our annual review, we were shamed for letting our labour costs rise above 12%.

"All departments need to cut back their hours," our new GM told us.

Always the voice of dissent, I tried to point out how challenging this was going to be.

"Are we going to get less product? We're already struggling to get items on the floor fast enough. And now we have to cull even more hours?"

"You'll have to find a way to make it work," she said.

"I'm not a math genius, but I'm pretty sure it's impossible for a mere mortal to process 100 units per minute." Imagine baking 100 cookies from scratch in one minute. Or sending 100 tweets in 60 seconds.

I had zero support from my fellow managers. My GM lifted her arms, palms out like wings, and shrugged. This was the way she expressed three things:

- It's not my decision.
- I'm powerless to do anything.
- It's not my problem, it's yours.

I would try to develop a plan where we could achieve these unrealistic goals. I would have a meeting with the staff who would echo my own objections. I would open my arms and shrug, mimicking our general manager.

As a retail manager, I never worked on commission and I never worked for a company that paid its employees that way. My father worked in commission-based sales for a good portion of his career and he shared stories of fellow staff stealing customers the minute his back was turned. Once he became a store manager, he tried to address that, but there was really no stopping it. Commission-based work is a bloodbath. It also offers no stability nor a guarantee of income. Even though retail management salaries are often paltry, at least I had the promise of a steady paycheque.

As a young, career-driven woman living on my own, I managed to pay my bills. I budgeted based on priority. Rent, groceries, gas, cable, and insurance were non-negotiable. I was not saving money for my future. I relied heavily on my credit cards. I knew better than to ever take out a cash advance and budgeted tightly in order to avoid that kind of debt. Selling books for a living wasn't going to make me wealthy, but I was living an adult life. Even if I had to give up meat for a while, I was happy living on my own.

Whenever I moved to a new company, I blindly accepted the salary I was offered. Being young and inexperienced, I never knew I could negotiate. I wouldn't have had the confidence to ask for more money anyway. When my rent increased, I was forced to take on a second job in order to make ends meet. This was a hard pill to swallow. I was working full-time in management, but still needed a part-time job to cover the basics.

Despite the financial stress, I loved my job. I had wonderful staff working in my departments. I had control of what books were on the shelves. I built relationships with agents from the publishing companies, ensuring I was able to secure stock of the bestsellers when all other stores could not. The low balance in my bank account was offset by the fulfillment I felt every day I went to work.

10

The Gorilla in the Bookstore

Maybe it makes me a weirdo, but I loved being assigned as manager-on-duty, or MOD, in my bookstore. Each shift—there was an opening and closing shift—had an assigned MOD who responded to all managerial issues as they arose. While it took me away from my usual duties, I understood why this was a necessary role. Employees knew who to call for assistance, approvals, and guidance, and it gave me the opportunity to be exposed to departments I otherwise would have no reason to visit. I could stretch my managerial wings. In the two-storey Toronto store there were five managers, and MOD duties landed in my lap at least twice per week.

One afternoon, when I was the manager-on-duty for the day, I was paged to the music area. As I made my way through the store to the music lounge, I could hear a booming voice berating one of my staff. A man was demanding to speak to a manager. His aggression drowned out the gentle jazz being piped through the overhead speakers. I heard the unmistakable pound of a fist on the counter. My heart mimicked this with its own pounding. As I approached the section—up three steps at the back of the second floor, next to the coffee shop—I saw the man before he saw me. He was a six-foot-four gorilla of a man and he was raging like a silverback.

"WHERE IS IT?" he shouted at the employee behind the counter. Grayson, who worked full-time in this department, had put as much room between himself and the customer as possible. The circular cash, sales, and special order desk was in the centre of the shop. The only way Grayson could give this man some space was to stand in the middle. As I approached, I could see the discomfort on Grayson's face. I went into manager mode, intent on protecting my employee and finding a solution for this customer.

"Sir, how can I help you?" I said quietly, with a smile on my face. I was trying to diffuse the situation from the start with a friendly face, calming voice, and caring demeanour. I knew from prior experience that asking "What seems to be the problem?" is an antagonistic approach and not helpful when a customer is agitated from the start.

He whipped his body away from the desk, giving me a head-to-toe assessment.

"WHO THE HELL ARE YOU?" he bellowed.

"I'm the manager. How can I help you?"

"YOU CAN FIND MY GODDAMNED CD, THAT'S HOW!"

I glanced at Grayson, who shook his head.

"THIS MORON SAYS IT'S NOT HERE." He lunged at Grayson, who took a defensive step back.

"It still shows on order," Grayson said quietly from the safety of the centre of the desk.

My agenda pivoted from trying to find a resolution to getting this man off the sales floor, away from the customers who were watching the spectacle. In the 10 seconds I engaged with him, I realized he was a loose cannon. I wanted to pull him into an area where we could have a private—and hopefully calmer —conversation.

"Sir, why don't you come with me and we'll sort this out?" I gestured for him to follow me. We moved to the hallway outside the office I shared with my fellow department managers and my store manager.

Even though I had taken the lead, I deferred to his size and his rage. I recognized that any wrong move on my part would only further enrage him. When we came to a stop in front of the manager's office, he positioned himself in front of me, backing me against the wall. I fought the impulse to cross my arms. Instinctively, I wanted to protect myself, but I feared the posture would be misinterpreted as a challenge.

"Sir, why don't you tell me what happened."

"WHAT HAPPENED IS MY CD IS NOT FUCKING HERE!"

I put my hands out in front of me, trying to claim some personal space.

"You don't need to yell. I'm here to help. When did you order the CD?"

"FIFTEEN WEEKS AGO! FIFTEEN FUCKING

WEEKS! YOUR PEOPLE TOLD ME IT WAS GONNA BE TWO TO THREE WEEKS."

"Sir, I apologize for that, but sometimes we can't control distribution. I'll personally follow up and get some answers for you."

This man was so angry, he stopped hearing what I was saying.

"GO GET MY FUCKING CD YOU FUCKING TWAT!"

For the next 10 minutes, I was subjected to a misogynistic attack and called more foul names, all shouted into my face from the man towering over me. About halfway through the verbal bashing, I stopped listening. All I could focus on was the finger pointed in my face and the very large fist it was attached to. I suddenly found myself deathly afraid of this man, realizing his massive hands could easily wrap around my neck and squeeze. I simply stood there, shaking and praying that the three other managers on the other side of the office door would come help me. Not one did. I thought maybe they couldn't hear what was happening.

When the man finally stormed away, spent of his rage, and still unhappy and disgusted, I went to the bathroom, hid in a stall, and tried to calm my shaking. When I returned to the office to get my purse, not one of my colleagues could look me in the eye. The three of them sat at their desks, absorbed by whatever was on their computer screens. I stood there for a moment, stunned by their silence. No one said a word or acknowledged what had just happened. I felt my own anger bubbling inside me. Two young ladies passed by the other side of the office door. I heard their giggling, confirming there was no way in hell my colleagues hadn't heard what had transpired on the other side of that door. My heart broke a little.

"I'm not feeling well," I said. "I'm going home." I was still shaking, still in shock.

I went to check on Grayson, who had already made some calls to find the missing CD.

"I'm sorry he said those things to you," Grayson said to me. In the chaos, it had never occurred to me that everyone on the second floor of the store could hear the screaming.

"I was about to call 911 when I saw him leaving. Anyways, the CD is stuck at customs. Should I call him and leave a message?"

I shook my head. "No, pass this on to Marcus. This has to be escalated to him. It's a general manager thing now. I'm not ever dealing with that man again and neither are you."

I left the store in the middle of my shift. That night, alone in my apartment, I went through a range of emotions. Now that I was removed from the situation, my whole body started shaking. I cried. I ate my dinner and threw it up. I got angry at being left out there alone. No one had come to my aid. I gaslit myself, thinking maybe the situation wasn't as bad as I thought it was when it was happening.

Grayson's words came back to me. *I was about to call 911.* I wasn't crazy or being sensitive. This man had threatened my life and my 19-year-old employee was prepared to take more action than a team of managers who were all in their 30s.

I called in sick the next day. And then the day after that. When I returned to the store, I saw my colleagues in a completely different light. I mustered the courage to raise the issue a week after the incident during a management meeting.

"How come no one came to help me last week?"

My question was met with silence.

The general manager shuffled the papers in his hands. The operations manager turned his attention to a computer. The two other zone managers looked at each other and then at the floor. One of them hadn't been working that day, but I suspected she had been filled in.

"There's no way you couldn't hear what was happening on the other side of that door. Everyone heard that man threatening me."

Silence.

"It's nice to know you all have my back." I couldn't help myself. "I thought we were a team. My mistake."

I stood up from my chair and walked out of the office. The relationship was forever fractured, in my view. From that day forward, I withdrew from trying to be friends with any of them. I spoke to them only when necessary. When they tried to engage in chit chat with me, I delivered simple answers. They didn't deserve more than that. I still loved my job and held no grudge against the employees. I still carry the trauma of what happened to me that day, consciously avoiding corners where my back would be against the wall.

That gorilla of a man gave me the opportunity to dig

deep into how I managed difficult customers. In my head, I played out scenarios of what I could have done differently to avoid the dangerous situation. The next time I encountered an unreasonably irate customer, I called for the store manager to take it on. If he or she wasn't on duty that day, I made sure the issue was handled on the sales floor, where I had witnesses. I felt safer out in the open. Retail employees deal with angry customers every single day. When someone in a store is losing it, it's about something else in their life: an abusive spouse, a lost job, a stack of issues piling up on a person to the breaking point. It's never about the CD or the dry-clean-only blouse that shrunk in the wash, but simply at that moment, in your store, they reached their last thread.

Seven months after the incident, I was recruited by Old Navy. They asked me to disclose my current salary and then offered me $15,000 more per year than I was currently making. To a young woman who was barely making ends meet, this was a very big carrot. The timing was perfect, too. My annual performance review had taken place less than three weeks prior to this offer and I was disappointed about not receiving any raise at all. My general manager told me I wasn't working to my full potential, that I needed to work on my leadership skills and be more of a team player. The words stung deeply. This was the same place where all my "teammates" hid behind a closed door while I was being physically threatened by a customer on the other side. Needless to say, I was not deeply in love with my workplace.

Offer from Old Navy in hand, I approached my store manager and told him about it. I wanted to stay in the book business, and I was willing to tolerate a garbage review and a shitty team in exchange for more money. A day later, I was informed the company would match the offered salary.

I went home and had multiple conversations in my head. *Why did they so easily match this? Why wasn't I worth this amount before I was threatening to leave? Would things get better or worse now that I forced their hand?*

I took my day off to contemplate. I made a list of pros and cons. I considered my time with the company. I was clearly not valued for what mattered to me. I was passed over for promotion more than once. I was sent to a different store to train a new general manager, but not offered that position myself. My staff were brilliant, but the management team—from head office to the store level—soured the experience.

I pored over the offer from Old Navy, looking for an excuse to pass. The lure of the money and the opportunity to start fresh with a venture newly in Canada won. I left the job I loved, and despite the heartache, I still tell anyone to this day that it was the best job I ever had.

11

Fight Club 2000

My second retail management job put me smack dab in the middle of the fashion world—kind of. I was hired by Gap Inc. as a merchandising manager for Old Navy. The discount fashion chain wasn't slated to open in Canada until the spring of 2001, so from October through Christmas season 2000, all new managers would be training in Gap stores across Canada. Then, in January 2001, we would be sent to Old Navy stores in the United States for a further three months of operations and merchandising training. But for starters, I was assigned to a Gap store in the same mall where the Old Navy store I'd be working in was being built.

I had always had an arms-length view of The Gap, first as a fat kid, then as a poor one. When the first Gap store in Canada opened in a nearby mall when I was a kid, my girlfriends were over the moon excited about exploring this American brand, but I was nervous. I was chubby and typically clothes that my friends wore did not fit me. In the 1980s, the store represented everything a Canadian teenager wanted, but was out of reach unless you went to the United States: comfortable clothes worn by movie stars (Michael J. Fox made the pocket tee famous in *Back to the Future*), an iconic American brand, and a wall of blue jeans such as we'd never seen before.

We stood in line for almost an hour on the second weekend The Gap was open. When we reached the front, I was separated from my three friends who were admitted by the cute guy at the door.

"Sorry," he said holding his hand up to stop me. "You have to wait until someone comes out. Fire code, ya know?" He showed me a small metal device in his hand. His thumb twitched and I heard a click. I understood it was a counter and he was counting bodies.

From the other side of the glass doors, I watched my friends huddle together in front of the wall of blue jeans. They were pointing and nodding and touching and holding jeans up to their waists, completely oblivious that I wasn't with them. My heart cracked a little at being so invisible and easily forgotten.

"First time in The Gap?" the boy at the door asked.

I nodded shyly. Cute boys didn't talk to me, a 14-year-old chub with a bad perm.

"It's a fun place. What do you have your eye on?"

"Don't know," I muttered, staring at my off-brand runners.

"You should check out the ribbed sweaters. They're on a table at the back. Totally rad."

I found the courage to look up and smile at him.

"Thanks." I took in his chiseled cheekbones, seeing a hint of Rob Lowe in him. He *was* super cute.

When a group of girls burst out of the store, bags in hands, excitedly chatting about what they would wear to school on Monday, cute door guy let me pass into the holy land.

The spotlights were bright, pointed with intention toward the wall of jeans to my left, and the T-shirts stretched into shadow boxes on the wall to my right. They shone on posters of perfect-bodied women and men. I moved to the jeans, scanning from top to bottom, trying to make sense of the different styles and cuts. At the top, near the ceiling, I could see size 2. My eyes travelled down the wall, through 4, 6, 8, 10, and stopping at the bottom at 12. I was a generous 14. I leaned back, turning my head to follow the wall stretching to the back of the store, hoping to find plus size there. The wall was split in two: women's at the front, men's at the back. There was nothing to fit me in denim.

I moved on to the T-shirts, finding an extra-large that might fit. On the table, the T-shirts were displayed like the colours of a rainbow. Shades of red fanned out into shades of violet. It was gorgeous. My eyes were pulled to the tables and racks of perfectly folded, hung, and co-ordinated clothing. This was where the seed was planted for my love of merchandising.

I looked at the price of the deep purple pocket tee I was holding. Eight dollars. I didn't have that kind of money. I was used to buying my clothes in the discount department store where eight bucks would buy me two tees, a three-pack of underwear, and a bra that would stretch out of shape after six washes.

The ribbed sweater the door boy told me to look at was $12. The extra-large was huge and roomy and exactly what I would have loved to wear to hide my bulges. I wished I had the money to buy one. It could be the one item of brand clothing that I would own. I was grateful that my friends had abandoned me and wouldn't be witness to my disappointment.

I spotted my friends over by the fitting room, waiting in line with armloads of clothing to try. I was happy for them, a whole lot jealous, and calculating how many hours of babysitting it would take to save up for a sweater, bus fare, and lunch at the mall. While I couldn't buy anything that day, I thought maybe one day in the near future I would.

All these memories came rushing back to me the first morning I walked under the updated logo of Gap. Now I was thinner, richer, and knew what kind of jeans I could rock.

On that first day, I was welcomed with open arms. I was given my employee card and my discount and told to go ahead and shop for some basics. Our discount gave us 50% off three items every month and 30% off the rest. We were required to wear only Gap clothing and this was a way to make it affordable. I loaded up with denim, sweaters (it was October), and a few tees.

By mid-afternoon, I was ingrained with the culture of Gap. Have fun, keep things tidy, customers first. I met the district manager, Greg, who specifically came in to meet me and welcome me to the company.

Greg walked the store with me, explaining the merchandising concepts in play. He showed me the proper way to fold denim (if you thought folding a fitted sheet was brutal, watch how Gap employees purposefully fold blue jeans), taught me about size runs, and how to fold sweatshirts so the full logo was always visible.

"I encourage my managers to try new things," Greg said, flattening the inseam crotch of a pair of women's skinny jeans. "Be adventurous with your merchandising. Know your customer."

"This is a lot to take in. I hope I get it right. I struggle with matching socks in my own laundry," I joked.

Greg laughed, handing me a pair of flares to fold.

"We're not saving the world, Dana. We're selling blue jeans."

In those short sentences, Greg shattered my illusions about the brand, knocking it off the pedestal 14-year-old me had placed it upon. It was the most valuable lesson I would ever learn in retail. He was telling me to never forget what I was really doing for a living. There is no glamour and no space for ego.

When the Christmas season started during the first week of November, I was excited about the new lines, including sparkly sweaters and velvet five-pocket pants that I bought with my 50% discount. I was slim enough to wear a girls' size 14 top, which was smaller than the extra-large women's tee I couldn't fit into in 1984. While I was curvy, at least when I looked at the marketing posters, I knew I could wear what the models were wearing. I was having fun every day, too; learning lights me up, especially when it concerns merchandising. A perfectly folded wall of denim calmed me and gave me a deep sense of satisfaction at the same time. It looked great and was easy to shop without any anxiety. A well-built display of sweaters and vests told a visual story about a lifestyle, and I knew it could trigger desire. "I want to look like that," was an internal message I had carried around since I was a kid.

The store was a constant hub of activity. Sales were brisk, customers were demanding, and employees were burning out all around me. I was revelling in all the action, like a honeymooner in love. The churn of product and people was like nothing I had ever experienced. Christmas at Chapters was never frenzied. Sure, the lines at the cash register were long, but buying books lacked the urgency of immediate need I was seeing in play at Gap.

When Christmas Eve rolled around, I knew I was in for a long night. As the only Jewish manager, I volunteered to work the shift, closing the store, papering the front windows with brown kraft to hide the activity, and pricing every item in store for the Boxing Day sale. The biggest sale day of the year—Canada's equivalent of Black Friday in the United States—requires a lot of preparation.

My team for this task was every other Jew who worked in the store: two full-timers and six part-timers.

"I need your guidance here," I told Jeannie, the full-time merchandising associate who had been in the store for four years. "How does this normally roll out?"

"First, we order."

"Order?"

"Dinner. Chinese food."

Of course we do. Almost every Jewish family I knew spent Christmas Eve eating Chinese food and watching *Frosty the Snowman* or *The Wizard of Oz*.

Jeannie went to the central cash area, dug in a drawer and pulled out the menu for the restaurant across the parking lot. Everyone picked a dish and I sent two employees to get the food, drinks, paper plates, and cutlery.

We converted an oversized display table into a dining table by piling all the sweaters covering it onto the floor. We ate, sitting cross-legged on the floor, leaning against the blue jean wall or the papered windows. I asked the staff questions about their lives, their families, and their schools. The mood was festive and jovial. It was going to be a long night, but a fun one. There would be no customers to deal with. I imposed no rules other than we needed to get the job done. When we were done eating, we got to work. I had price sheets in hand, assigning each employee a section to price. For the rest of the night, the non-Christmas music blared, drowning out the incessant clicking and ticking of the pricing guns. When every item had its new sticker, we cleaned up, re-folded, re-signed, and picked up errant little white stickers off the floor. When we wrapped up, it was just past 2 a.m. I reminded the employees to check their schedule for Boxing Day because it would be all hands on deck. Start time: 6 a.m.

for management, 7 a.m. for employees. Doors opened at eight.

I spent most of Christmas Day sleeping in, reading a book, and smoking cigarettes. I was up at 4:30 a.m. on Boxing Day, ready and excited for the energy of the day. When I arrived at the store, our store manager was already there, checking the overnight reports for any late price changes and confirming that the point of sale software was showing the new discounts. I took up the new price sheets and began checking accuracy. As my fellow managers arrived, they took the sheets for their departments and did the same. At 7 a.m., the employees were directed to re-price things that had changed or that we had missed.

At 7:30 a.m., Greg whooshed into the store. His messenger bag was slung over his right shoulder and rested on his left hip. He was hugging a bag of popcorn that stretched from his kneecaps to the top of his head.

"IT'S SHOWTIME!" he yelled. "Are you ready?" he asked me.

"I'm ready," I confirmed. "I love it when it's busy."

"Busy," he laughed. "Oh, it's not just busy. It's chaos. It's crazy. It's fight club."

"Fight club? What do you mean?"

"Oh, you'll see," he smiled. "Popcorn'll be in the back. I've got cups in my bag for filling." I smiled back. I felt like I was about to be initiated into a private society. I wanted to ask him more questions, but I knew the first rule of fight club is you don't talk about fight club.

Greg came back out to the floor, gave us an inspiring speech, thanked us all for being here and being part of the best team in the district, and reminded us to take all our scheduled breaks. He then walked to the windows at the front of the store and began pulling the paper off.

Like a character in a movie who has just discovered the end of the world as she knew it outside her home, I walked slowly to the windows. The crowd was bunched up in front of the doors, like zombies trying to get at our brains—if zombies wore yoga pants and drank Starbucks. I had never seen anything like it in real life.

When we unlocked the glass doors, Greg held them closed against the sea of bodies. He held a hand up to the people and told them to back up just a little so we could swing the doors out. The doors could open inwards or outwards. Most days they were opened to the inside, but for Boxing Day, every bit of space counted and those doors needed to be out, sitting flush against the display windows. There was a pause in the thrum outside the store until he started pushing the doors. I jumped out of the way as the first customer pushed her way through the 10-inch gap between the two doors. And then the dam burst.

People flooded the store in a frenzy. They pulled velvet pants and jeans off the shelves. Grown adults were tossing T-shirts in the air like confetti at a wedding. Women yelled across piles of sparkling sweaters, asking their friends what size they needed. Employees were accosted as soon as they emerged from the stockroom, arms loaded with merchandise. Jeannie came onto the floor with a stack of girls' denim in each arm. She winked at me through the grill on the football helmet she was wearing. Somewhere in the kids section, a child cried.

It was apocalyptic and I couldn't wipe the smile off my face. It was 8:04 a.m.

As I stood just inside the front doors taking in the mayhem, Greg sidled up to me and handed me a cup of popcorn.

"Come with me," he said. "I know the best seats to watch the show."

I followed him to the front of the women's section. We stood with our backs to the mall entrance, watching the horde pull apart our store. I glanced at Greg who was tossing popcorn into his mouth with a crooked smile on his face.

Before I could ask him what he meant about the show, the yelling started. Two women stood at the display table where we'd eaten our Chinese food buffet. Each had a hand on a single sweater in the midst of a full-out tug-of-war. The sweater was wrenched back and forth as they screamed like toddlers on the playground.

"I had my hand on it first!"

"No, I did!"

"You weren't even here. You were on the other side of the table!"

"Are you blind? I was standing here the whole time."

"Do you think I'm stupid? I already had this in my hand."

I started to move forward, intending to stop the argument and find another sweater in the stockroom.

Greg's arm shot out in front of me, like a mother who brakes suddenly and is trying to protect a child sitting in the front seat of a car. He shook his head.

"Just wait," he whispered.

"This sweater is mine, bitch," the one on the left said, giving the sweater a hard pull.

I swear the other woman's eyes momentarily rolled into the back of her head. I saw white; she clearly saw red. In slow motion, the woman on the right raised her free hand and swiped at her opponent, landing an open palm slap to the face. In a flash there was screaming, hair pulling, punching, kicking, and an attempt at biting.

All over a 60/40 rayon/polyester sweater that was going to pill after 30 minutes of being worn.

We didn't need to intervene. We had security posted at the entrance to the store and they were there in a hurry. They tried to pull the two women apart, but they were tethered by their iron grips on the sweater. They were still yelling at each other, saying things no woman should ever say to another woman, especially not over synthetic fibres.

Calmly, and no longer wearing her football helmet, Jeannie walked into the fray, a pair of scissors in her hand. She reached between the warring women and snipped at the sweater's neckline.

"Noooo!" screamed one.

"What are you doing?" yelled the other.

Each woman gave another yank on the sweater. Jeannie was still cutting and then the sweater gave up the fight, ripping neatly in half.

"Now both of you have the sweater," Jeannie said before walking away.

The women were stunned into silence and security escorted them out of the store.

I watched Jeannie sashay her way to the back, scissors over her head like a trophy. She was going to be a great mother someday.

The two halves of the sweater were now on the floor. I picked them up to take them to the back so I could log the loss.

"Come back when you're done," Greg called after me. "We can watch the next event in babyGap."

12

Sorry, Who are You?

I had been counting down the days until my departure for training in America. Since I had worked Christmas Eve, I was off for New Year's Eve. I was also given a day off in lieu for working Boxing Day, so I had three days to decide what I'd be taking with me. My fiancé and I spent New Year's Eve alone at my request. I was going to be gone for three months and wanted him to myself.

"Why don't we just pop into the party for a few minutes?" he implored as we opened up our take-out containers.

"I don't really feel like getting dressed up and putting on makeup," I explained. We had been invited to two parties, both friends of his.

"You don't have to—"

"I know," I cut him off, "because I'm naturally beautiful and the life of the party no matter how I'm dressed." I grinned as I shoved a french fry into my mouth.

"I was going to say that no one would notice, but sure, go with that."

I dropped into a dining room chair, keeping my eyes on my quarter chicken dinner. Maybe three months apart would be good for our relationship. I was hoping the time and space would help him realize he could be nicer to me.

Regardless of his mood, I was very excited about the new adventure awaiting me. I was also very much looking forward to the larger salary that would enable me to pay rent and all my other expenses, as well as being able to save money and have meat in the freezer again. I'd been in retail long enough to know the promise of "the opportunity to grow" Old Navy spun during the recruitment process was probably empty and really meant "If you toe the company line and never protest, you might get your own store one day." Under those terms, I was going to be in middle management forever. But at least now, I'd be paid a little better.

While in the United States, we would have accommodations and a daily stipend, and we would learn everything from operations to merchandising. At the mass orientation in Canada, we were handed a sheet where we could indicate what states we wanted to go to.

"Please list your top three," the human resources person from the San Francisco head office said. "We cannot guarantee that you'll end up there, but we will do our best to fulfill the requests."

I gave this serious thought. The plan was to spend

January to March in the United States. As a girl who grew up with the frigid winters of Toronto, the first place that came to mind was Florida. Spend three months away from a Canadian winter? Okay, sign me up. Without access to a computer (this was before smartphones), I had to guess at which of the warmest states had a high number of stores. It stood to reason, in my mind, that I would have a better shot of being sent to a store in the Sunshine State than Hawaii.

I eliminated New Orleans and Georgia because the sticky humidity I had read about in many novels was not appealing. I know, Florida is just as bad, but I knew it well, having visited every winter break from the age of eight to 14. My second choice was California, and for my third, I selected Washington, because I had heard winters were mild in the Pacific Northwest.

All the managers-to-be were currently scattered for training at Gap stores throughout Ontario, spread out like seeds being planted for the next wave of growth. We wouldn't know where we were going until the first week of January.

As I learned how to fold blue jeans, how to submit daily reports, and the basics of Gap Inc. operations, I dreamed about spending my off time on a beach in Miami. I envisioned hiking the hills of northern California. I thought about walking through downtown Seattle without a heavy winter parka.

I tore my envelope open when it arrived at the Gap store where I was training. I scanned the letter, looking for my assigned store. It was at the bottom of the page along with the address and the store manager and district manager's names. I was heading to…

Illinois.

What?

My Saturday afternoon beach fantasy crumbled. I had never been to Illinois, but I knew one thing for sure. It was fecking cold in the winter.

"Where the heck is Bloomington?" I said aloud to no one in particular.

When I got home, I fired up MapQuest. If you throw a dart at a map of Illinois, the bull's-eye is Bloomington. More than two hours away from Chicago. Population about 65,000. In contrast, Toronto at the time had a population of 2.4 million.

Every stereotype I carried within me about small-town living filled my mind. I had never spent any significant time in a small town, other than an afternoon wine tour in Niagara-on-the-Lake, so my knowledge was coloured by free samples of ice wine. Still, I pictured farmers in overalls. I envisioned being stared at like an exotic bird. I worked on clever answers to curious and ignorant questions about Canada. I suspected Saturday night at Wal-Mart was the most stimulating place to be. Still, I was excited to be living in a furnished apartment, to have a rental car, and to be near enough to Chicago to get some great shopping in. From my Torontonian point of view, America was the land of the clearance sale and outlet malls, where I once bought Birkenstocks for $11 and a TAG Heuer watch for $79.99.

Five days before a slew of Canadian retail managers

was to descend on Old Navy stores across the United States, we were called to an all-hands meeting in a rented conference room at a hotel in the Toronto suburbs. It was there we met our colleagues—the ones we would be travelling and working with at our stores. My partner was Carly, a petite and enthusiastic woman. She was bouncing on her tiptoes, her personality bubbling out. She energized me and tired me out at the same time. We were equally excited about the upcoming adventure.

As we huddled awkwardly in the boardroom waiting for something to happen, we naturally compared notes. Carly and I moaned in unison when we met managers who were assigned to Florida, Texas, the Carolinas, and, yes, Hawaii.

"You are really lucky," Carly responded as each warm location was revealed. My internal response was a bit different: *I hate you right now.*

When we were asked where we were going, I had to explain where Bloomington was. Carly had not bothered to investigate where we would be living for the next three months. In a juvenile attempt to make the small city sound better, I always added we were "near Chicago." Carly was so excited about the whole journey and experience. I wasn't going to be the one to burst her bubble. Truthfully, some of her enthusiasm was rubbing off on me. By the end of that meeting, I convinced myself that this was going to be a great opportunity.

We flew from Toronto to Bloomington–Normal Central Illinois Regional Airport with an hour-long stopover in Atlanta. That means we flew 1,531 kilometres south to then fly 1,075 kilometres north to get to a destination that was 995 kilometres west of where we started. This kind of re-routing was shortly going to become the norm for Carly and me.

We spent our flights and waiting time getting to know each other. Carly had come from the same company my fiancé worked for and she knew him— proof, again, of how small the retail world can be. We talked about our career goals, shared stories of hilarious customer interactions, and swapped personal details.

"I hope the nightlife is good," she said, "because I love to dance. That's my cardio."

The large yellow kraft envelopes we each had contained everything we needed for this part of the trip: papers stating we would be working in the United States but be paid by a Canadian company, reservations for the car rental, the store address, the name of the district manager, the address of our apartment building, and a pre-loaded Visa card for our per diem.

Either our district manager or the store manager was going to greet us at the baggage claim, before we went to collect our cars. Then, Carly and I planned to drive to our apartment building, and maybe drive by the mall where the store was located. Our agenda was to drop our bags, hit up a restaurant for dinner, and then get groceries to carry us through the next week. Then back to our apartments to unpack and settle in.

The airport was nicer than I expected. Modern and clean with a gleaming granite floor. There were windows everywhere, offering great views of the snow-dusted tarmac. Darkness was just starting to settle in, but I could see a US Air Force plane and a Gulfstream private jet parked outside.

I went outside to have a smoke while we waited for our bags to come around the carousel. The frozen wind slapped me in the face and made my nose hairs stick together. I huddled inside my winter jacket, realizing the synthetic filling was inadequate against the cold. A digital scrolling sign hanging above me told me it was 6:43 p.m., January 11, 2001, current temperature 32 degrees Fahrenheit. I was starting to learn about the power of the wind in Illinois.

When I was back in the lobby, I scanned the area, looking for someone holding a piece of paper with our names written in bold, black marker. Being a regional airport, the foot traffic was light and we could see clear to the outside, where taxis, limousines, and a beat-up Pontiac waited for their passengers. We watched people come and go. I was getting hungry and quickly scanned the concourse for any open stores or fast-food kiosks. There was a sundries store selling magazines, drinks, snacks, and an assortment of travel accessories. I pivoted from the luggage carousel to the front doors to the shop, trying to decide what to do. By the time I decided to dash over to try grabbing a Snickers bar, the woman working the shop was pulling the shuttered doors across the front, closing up for the night.

It took less than 10 minutes for our bags to emerge from the plastic flap at the far end of the carousel. The plane from Atlanta to Bloomington had been a small commuter plane, filled mostly with business people travelling with carry-on luggage. I counted 11 bags, including our two, on the baggage carousel.

The lobby emptied out; the Pontiac and limos had pulled away. There were two taxis still waiting at the curb. There was no sign of anyone looking for two travel-weary, but still excited, retail managers from Canada.

"Do you think they forgot about us?" Carly asked.

I shook my head. "How can you forget about two people coming from another country? Maybe they're just late."

Warning Sign #1: If someone isn't at the airport on time to greet you, they aren't that interested.

"What should we do?"

"Wait, I guess."

We sat on a bench, facing the front doors. My stomach rumbled with hunger and I heard Carly's do the same. As we sat there, confused and worried, the hunger pains turned to anxious gurgles.

"Maybe we should call Mel," I suggested a half hour later. Mel was our district manager in Ontario, but without any stores yet to manage, she had been given the duty of managing the travel and acting as liaison for all the travelling managers.

I opened my flip phone, hesitant to make the call. I had limited long-distance minutes. I was relieved—but disturbed—when her voicemail clicked on. It was already almost 9 p.m. Eastern time, 8 p.m. Central for us. I could leave a message and not have to eat up my minutes in a conversation.

"Hi Mel, it's Dana and Carly calling from Bloomington, Illinois. We are at the airport," I turned my body to look behind me, "actually we are the only ones at this airport and no one is here to greet us." My voice warbled, and I fought back the tears. "We're not sure what to do. I hope you get this message and call me back."

I closed my phone and looked at Carly.

"How long do we wait for a call back?" I asked.

"Let's give her a half hour. If we don't hear back, we'll get our cars and figure out how to get to the apartment."

We sat in silence, lost in our thoughts. I flipped my phone open more than once to make sure it was charged and working. My phone rang at 8:27 p.m. local time.

"Hey," Mel said. "I am so sorry this happened. There was some kind of mix-up about who was supposed to come get you. I spoke to the DM and he said he's sending one of the other store managers to come greet you. Someone will be there in the next half hour or less." I liked Mel. She took action and found the solution before calling back. From the first day I met her, I knew she was one of those people who came to the table with answers.

"Maybe we'll get our rental cars sorted out in the meantime," I suggested. "Then we'll be ready to follow whoever comes to meet us."

"Yeah, do that," Mel agreed. "Good plan. Call me back when someone gets there."

I filled Carly in on the plan and we walked over to the car rental area. It was fully abandoned. No customers, no staff at the counters. We were greeted by a plastic CLOSED sign sitting on the counter. Below the word closed was the line "WILL BE BACK AT" with a clock, its small red hands moved to indicate 9:30.

"What the…" I pressed my lips together, pissed that we had to wait another hour for the agent to return.

"Do you need some help?" A voice came from behind us.

I turned to see a security guard approaching.

"We're supposed to pick up rental cars," I answered.

"They all close by 8 or 8:30," he said, "unless you're with that one down there," he pointed with his chin. "They close at 4."

"This sign says they'll be back at 9:30," Carly said.

"In the morning. You ladies need to find another ride tonight."

Carly and I looked at each other for a moment, stunned. We thanked the man and walked back to the main lobby, back to our bench.

At 9 p.m. on the dot, I called Mel again, telling her no one had yet arrived and the car rental was closed.

Warning Sign #2: If someone says they'll do something and they don't, they're not forgetful, they've put their priorities elsewhere.

"Hmmm, weird," she muttered. "Just take a taxi to your building. Get the receipt and I'll reimburse you."

We walked out of the airport more than two hours after we arrived. A single taxi waited at the curb. We got in and gave the driver the address of our destination. The exhaustion and stress of the day were settling into my bones. I was looking forward to dumping my bags in my apartment and digging into salty, greasy fast food, a comfort in this unrest. Carly, who was just as worn down as I, emphatically agreed.

"Fries with gravy sounds perfect right now," she said.

We drove for about 10 minutes, when the driver pulled into the parking lot of a hotel.

"This can't be right," I muttered.

"That's the address you gave me, miss. Is there somewhere else you want me to take you?"

I shook my head and Carly and I unfolded ourselves from the back of the cab, then pulled our enormous suitcases out of the trunk. It had gotten much colder since we first arrived at the airport, but my face was flushed and the cold was helping to calm my nerves.

Inside the lobby, we were greeted by a sole woman at the registration counter. We approached, told her we had a reservation.

"Do you have your confirmation number?"

Carly and I were pulling papers from our envelopes, scanning the pages for a confirmation number. I didn't see one, and neither did Carly, but we didn't trust that our weary brains were functioning properly. One thing we both clearly remembered: we were promised furnished apartments, not a hotel room.

"We can't seem to find one," Carly said.

"Not a problem." The woman smiled. "We can find it with your last names."

When the search for our last names yielded nothing, my stomach clenched and I felt my bowels tense up. My armpits got sweaty and for a second, my vision blurred.

Warning Sign #3: Your body knows shit is about to go sideways before your brain catches up.

I gave her Mel's first and last name. The district manager's name. Nothing.

"Try Old Navy," I suggested. Nothing.

"How about…" I looked for any other name on my mess of papers. "Old Navy, Eastland Mall?"

"No," the woman said, shaking her head. "Are you sure you're at the right place? There's another hotel right behind us."

I showed her the paper titled ACCOMMODATIONS with the address.

"That's our address all right. What kind of room do you think was booked?"

"A suite, I think," Carly answered. "For three months."

The woman's brow creased. "I can tell you for sure we don't have any long-term bookings. We also don't have any suites available for that period of time. I can, however, offer you a standard hotel room."

Sweat was now starting to form on my forehead. The idea of living in a hotel room without a kitchen was not comforting.

"Maybe we should call Mel again," Carly whispered. I nodded.

I made the call, not even worrying about the minutes. Mel answered. In my head, thoughts were clear and coherent, but what came out of my mouth was panic.

"Mel, we have no place to stay. We're at a hotel. No reservation. We're stranded. What do we do?"

Mel blew a puff of air through the handset.

"Let me think for a minute…"

"Think faster," I snapped. "We've been travelling for more than…" I looked at my watch, "12 hours. We're hungry and tired and this is ridiculous. How did this get so messed up?"

"I'll figure this out. I'll call you back." And she hung up on me.

The lady behind the counter, who looked to be our age, also hung up her phone.

"I called the Holiday Inn across the way. They have king suites available. With kitchenettes. I'll drive you over."

My brain was foggy as this lovely woman called someone to cover the front desk, walked us to her car, and drove us to a competitor. I remembered to thank her, but neglected to get her name so I could call her boss and praise her efforts to help us.

The man at the registration desk at the Holiday Inn was waiting for us. He smiled as he took our names, gave us keys, and welcomed us to what would be our home for the next 91 days.

"My name is Emmett," he said. "Please let me know what else I can do for you."

I gave him a thin smile, thanked him, and, with Carly trailing behind me, made my way to the elevators. I stopped, realizing there *was* something he could do for me.

"Is there room service here?"

Emmett shook his head. "Unfortunately, no. We have some snacks here in the pantry, if you'd like."

"Where's the best place to get a burger and fries?"

"Oh, that's easy. Mr. Quick. Or Bennigan's. But they are both closed now."

Of course they are.

"Is anything open?"

"Honey, you're in Bloomington. The only thing opened past 10 p.m. is the Wal-Mart across the street." And it wasn't even Saturday night.

I looked at Carly, who had pushed the button to summon the elevator.

"Looks like we're walking to the supercenter." She laughed and stepped into the elevator. I followed her in, pushing the button for our floor.

"Y'all be careful," Emmett called out from the desk. "Thursday night is fight night at Wal-Mart. You hear any shouting, you run from the gun."

The doors slid closed before I could ask him what he meant. Carly and I looked at each other and burst out laughing. Every other emotion had been spent.

Our sad dinner consisted of frozen entrées from Wal-Mart. The visions I had of cooking up chicken with pasta were squashed the minute I walked into my suite. We skipped the grocery shop, since our rooms had only a small fridge and a microwave.

The suite itself wasn't horrible. A one-bedroom, with a sliding door separating the bedroom from the living area. It was no frills, functional, and clean, and I sat on the couch, spooning my pitiful microwaved macaroni and cheese into my mouth. The salt was comforting, but the meal was tasteless.

How was I going to get through the next three months like this?

Carly knocked on my door shortly after 11 p.m.

"Did Mel call you again?"

I shook my head. It was past midnight in Toronto.

"I guess we'll speak to her tomorrow." It was more of a question than a comment.

I tossed my meal into the garbage as anger rose in me. *Why should she rest easy when Carly and I are in limbo here?*

So I called Mel again, but this time she didn't answer. I left a voice message telling her where we were, fighting hard to contain my anger and prevent the bitch in me from spewing forth.

"What time are we supposed to be at the store tomorrow?" I asked Carly. I rubbed my eyes, pushing back the fatigue and tears.

"11 a.m. We should get our cars, find a breakfast place. Want to go to the store in one car?"

I shook my head. "Nah. I want to figure out the route on my own. Let's meet in the lobby at eight."

Carly said goodnight and left. I turned on the TV, scrolled through channels, rage simmering in my chest. I blankly stared at an infomercial, feeling abandoned and lonely, but strangely excited for the next day. I was looking forward to learning how to manage and merchandise.

I called Emmett at the front desk and asked for a 7 a.m. wake-up call.

"Sleep well with sweet dreams. Things will be better in the morning."

His kind and caring words made me realize that in all the chaos, I had never once thought to call my fiancé to let him know I had arrived safely.

In the morning there was a message at the front desk for us. Leslie, the daytime desk clerk, was already well aware of our situation.

"Emmett told me what happened, but I want to make sure you know we are here to take care of everything you need." She was genuinely nice, a very welcome friendly face after an emotionally challenging day.

I unfolded the pink slip. The message was from Mel. I read it out loud.

"Sorry for the mix-up. You and Carly take yourselves out for a nice dinner and the company will pay for it."

Carly stepped behind me, reading the two sentences over my shoulder.

"That's it?" she hissed in my ear. "That's how they're going to deal with this?"

Bubbly and positive-thinking Carly evaporated.

"MOTHERFUCKING BULLSHIT!" she raged. "BUNCH OF ASSHOLES."

Warning Sign #4: When the calmest person in the room loses her shit, things are going to get worse.

The four people sitting in the breakfast area turned to see what all the yelling was about. I wasn't embarrassed; I was gleeful. I was enjoying seeing a side of Carly I didn't know existed.

"You know what we're going to do?" she continued. "We're going to find the most expensive restaurant here and we're going to order the most expensive items. And a vintage bottle of wine." She paused, then shook her head. "Fuckers."

Carly and I reported for duty at Eastland Mall well before 11 a.m. The stress from the last day was held at bay by a good breakfast of eggs and bacon. We were protein-packed and ready to take on the day.

"Hi! Welcome to Old Navy," said an energetic young man just inside the threshold. "Can I offer you a shopping bag?" He held out a blue mesh shoulder bag.

"Is the manager here?" I asked. "We're the managers from Canada."

"Uh, okay," he said. "I need a manager at the front."

I was about to confirm that was what I asked for when I noticed the headset nestled in his curly hair, a cushioned speaker over his ear, and a microphone curved toward his mouth.

Carly and I watched shoppers pick through T-shirts and look at tags for prices and sizes. A woman our age approached us, her shoulder-length, dirty blonde hair swinging with each step.

"Hi! I'm Sherie, one of the managers here. How can I help you?"

"We're the managers from Canada," Carly smiled, holding her hand out for a handshake.

Sherie looked at the outstretched hand. "Uh huh," she said.

We stood there awkwardly for a moment, not sure who was supposed to speak.

"We're starting our training today," I said, trying to be helpful.

"Uh huh," she uttered again. "For what?"

Carly and I looked at each other. It wasn't a glance, it was a pointed *Is this really fucking happening?* look.

"We're supposed to be training here for the next three months. For the stores in Canada?"

"Huh. Okay. I'll be right back."

We watched Sherie walk to the back of the store and vanish behind a door.

The curly headed boy with the bags smiled again. "Jeans for the whole family are the item of the week." He half-turned his body, pointing to a table piled with jeans for women, men, girls, and boys. "Let me know if you need me to find a size."

Before we could respond, he turned back to face the front of the store to greet the next customers.

"Hi! Welcome to Old Navy. Can I offer you a shopping bag?"

Carly and I walked through the store, examining the way things were merchandised. Metal hanging arms protruded from walls that were packed with items. It was a noticeable difference from the minimalist culture at Gap.

"Hi!" A voice surprised us from behind. "Are you the ones from Canada?"

In unison, we turned, nodding our heads.

"I'm Phillip, the store manager. I forgot you guys were coming. What are your names again?"

Warning Sign #5: If your host manager completely forgets you're coming to work in their store for three months AND cannot be bothered to remember your name AND doesn't bother telling the rest of their team, turn around and leave. Things will get much, much worse.

No one in the store knew we were coming. Not the other managers, not the staff. They were completely unprepared and uninterested in talking to us. That first day, we were planted in the lunchroom with a copy of the operations manual ("You guys can share, right?") and left to read it. Other employees barely acknowledged us, incurious about two strangers in their space. With a binder open between us and notebooks under our hands, they probably thought we were auditors.

After eight hours, I looked at Carly and said, "Do we just leave, or…?"

She shrugged. We emerged from the lunchroom, surprising the closing manager who was coming in. Turns out, Phillip and Sherie had left for the day without bothering to check in on us once or coming to say goodbye or letting us know what we would be doing the next day. We decided to be the stewards of our own training and shadow each manager on a rotating basis.

That night, Mel called as Carly and I sat down to dinner at a random steakhouse. We had already had our first sips of a $65 bottle of wine. Since neither of us were wine savvy, Carly scanned the prices on the wine list and pointed to the one with the highest price.

I put Mel on speaker.

"I'm sorry to say you'll be staying at the hotel for the duration," Mel told us. "The district manager forgot to book anything else for you. Are the hotel accommodations adequate?"

Carly and I exchanged a look. I didn't need a mirror to show me my face was reflecting the anger I saw in hers.

"We're going to need a bigger stipend," I blurted out. "With no kitchen, we'll have to eat out a lot."

"I'll see what I can do," Mel said. "Did you get my message about dinner?"

"We're at a restaurant right now," Carly said. "We just ordered some wine."

"Oh… uh… alcohol isn't covered. We… uh… don't pay for that."

Sometimes, the bitch in me will not be detained.

"Mel, you know what?" I said, keeping my voice as steady as I could. "You *will* pay for the wine. I don't care if it comes out of your own pocket. Somebody screwed up big time. Carly and I have to live in a hotel for three months, eating microwave meals and over-paying for laundry. No one at the store knew we were coming and they don't care that we're there. The least you can do is spring for a bottle of wine. You'll sleep better tonight knowing you at least allowed us this one little victory." Mel didn't argue.

At the end of that first week, we had a conference call with all the managers transplanted across the US. Some told stories of welcoming parties the staff threw for them on their first day. One store had a Canadian flag cake made. At the Austin location, staff had filled a wall in the breakroom with photos of everyone who worked in the store with cue cards featuring highlights about each of them. Many of our colleagues fielded endless questions about Canada, since most of the employees had never even travelled outside their own state. My hands balled into fists and Carly stared blankly at the bulletin board showing the sales numbers for the week.

When we left the store, the wind was biting, slapping my face. We really were in the coldest place on earth.

For the next three months, we learned as much as we could. We worked all shifts, making our own hours. Our fellow managers let us know when the big things were happening, like an entire new line coming in that required a whole section to be switched out. No one asked us over for dinner. No one engaged in conversation outside of work-related topics. It was weird. In the darkest days, I held onto my ambition to one day work at corporate head office.

The store manager also managed two other stores. We saw him three times over the course of our training. We never met the district manager. I took this as a sign that he was embarrassed about dropping the ball and didn't have the maturity to come meet us and apologize. I later learned it was a sign of a company whose upper management was deeply broken.

13

Never Pay Retail Again

E verything goes on sale eventually, and unless you've fallen into a bucket of ferret shit and need clothes in an emergency, as a retail employee you never have to pay full price for anything.

When I started at Old Navy in Bloomington in January, I had already missed the post-holiday markdowns—but those aren't the only deep discounts in retail. The store was being flooded with new stock and returns were coming in droves. This was where I discovered markdown glory. A shirt purchased in October and returned in January had already reached final clearance status. As a customer with a gift receipt, you will get the full paid value in the form of store credit or a gift card. As an employee, I'm salivating because I know when I go to reprice that item, it will now be well below the original price. Those cool jeans I couldn't afford at $49 were just returned in brand-new condition and can now be mine for $2.99. But before you mark your calendar and rush to shop for super cheap returned items after the holidays, you should know most of the returns won't make it back to the sales floor. This is one of the only golden tickets retail employees can cash in. We scoop up the goods, putting them aside for purchase at the end of our shifts.

My first markdown cycle at Old Navy happened while I was training in the Bloomington store. During our evening shift, we changed signage and moved things around to get ready for the sale the next day. We matched SKUs (stock-keeping units, also known as bar codes) on the tags hanging off the clothing to the numbers on our reports. In the morning, the opening manager would run the SKUs through the cash register to ensure the prices had been changed overnight in the software download. This was an onerous task, one that nobody wanted to do and that usually did not get finished before the doors opened for business. Naturally, this job was handed off to the lowest-ranking person—me—and presented as a "learning opportunity."

While retailers will operate on their own schedule for discounts, all goods will eventually be marked down. The language might be different, with catchphrases such as "price drop," "deal(s) of the week," "new lower price," "manufacturer's special," or "manager's special," to name a few. Markdowns will also happen on specific days of the week, and not all markdowns for all departments will happen at once. I've worked in stores where markdowns happen on Thursdays, or where women's clothing goes on sale on Tuesday, men's on Wednesdays. When I worked for Gap, the customers grew so savvy about when our markdowns happened (every two weeks on a Tuesday), the company had to switch the model and roll out markdowns on shifting days.

Most stores have a three-stage markdown. Stage 1 is generally 20% to 30%. Stage 2 will be 50% of the original price, and Stage 3 can be up to 75%. By the time items reach the third stage, the pickings are very slim and items will be shoved into a corner rack with FINAL CLEARANCE signs. Even then, that might not be the actual final clearance. Occasionally, there are further markdowns, but you'll need to be able to identify which items would fall into that category, since by this stage they typically won't be physically tagged.

If you are looking for a smoking deal on clothing, here are two things you can do:

1. Use your eyes. Scan for seasonal items or items that look out of place, such as a pattern that is vastly different from the rest. Channel your *Sesame Street* years: one of these things is not like the other, one of these things just doesn't belong. If the full spring line is out in store and already has some markdowns, scan the clearance area for things that don't fit the season. Flannels, wools, and dark colours fall into that category.

2. Learn to read the tags. Most manufacturers and companies date their lines. The hang tag might have that info, with full indications of what season the clothing comes from: fall,

spring, summer, winter, or holiday. Inside, the tag attached to the garment may have an abbreviated version of the season or it might have a month and date. I once bought a summer dress in the spring of 2017 with a label inside of 06/16. It was almost a year old and still on the clearance rack (see note about *Sesame Street*). Original price: $129. I paid $3.97. This doesn't happen often, but when it does, you will never forget it.

Another good time to score a deal is in late January or when labels with the letters DNI start showing up on displays and shelves. Those letters stand for Do Not

Inventory, and will let you know the store is preparing to take inventory. To the employees and management, that means hell is about to open her gates to an overwhelming workload, overnight hours, and lots of questions from loss prevention about how we allowed 97 parkas to be stolen. For the customers, inventory prep is an opportunity to get some phenomenal deals.

When I was a manager in a home goods store, the goal was to get rid of as many clearance items as possible. Scanning all the bits and bobs, odds and ends, and miscellany to be counted as inventory takes time. Many of the items don't have proper tags, so those need to be reprinted. In one of my brilliant (to me) ideas, I put all the crap on a rolling shelf rack, made up a dummy SKU (sometimes called a dump SKU) and printed a sign that said "All items $1.99." By the end of my shift, more than three-quarters of the items were sold, but I was getting shit for pushing the rack full of crap to the front of the store.

"This is not what we want people to see when they first come in," my manager explained to me, using a tone teachers reserved for instructing kindergarteners to share. "Walking in to a rack of clearance is not in line with our image."

I didn't argue. I thanked her for telling me that, and rolled the rack back to the stockroom. By that point in the game, I knew better than to point out the success. I knew there was no sense in telling her I cleared most of that shit out of the store in less than eight hours. In retail, a sensible choice that results in sales is irrelevant. But part of me really wanted to tell her that my gutsy move increased the UPTs (Units Per Transaction) for the day and made space for non-clearance items. Instead, I was told I needed to put all the remaining items back on the clearance shelves at the back of the store before I could leave for the day. It wasn't a big deal. What started as a mish-mash of items spread out over 15 short shelves at the end of five gondolas was now reduced to three shelves at the end of one of the fixtures. Despite being shot down, this was a very good day for me.

While I was training at Old Navy, I experienced firsthand the insanity of preparing for inventory. It was scheduled for the last two days of January, so we had the month to recover from holiday sales and returns before we needed to clean the store and organize, then empty, the overstocks—the space above the display for all the extra stock. The goal was to get as much stock onto the floor as possible. Nothing was kept in the back or in the receiving area. Everything was stored on the sales floor, hidden behind vinyl curtains we could flip up to access the excess.

In preparation, each evening we would flip over every curtain and replenish as much stock onto the sales floor as possible. Inventory is easier to count when it's not stacked and piled in overhead storage. One night, Carly and I were working in the kids' section, pulling out bulky sweaters, long-sleeved shirts with sparkly graphics, super soft fleece pyjamas, and flare jeans with embroidered embellishments.

"Holy, there's a lot of sweaters and shirts in here," Carly announced from the top of the ladder.

I craned my neck so I could see. The clothing was piled almost to the top of the storage area and out to the edges. There had to be hundreds of items in there and it was a mess. Nothing was folded and everything had been shoved into the space.

"Okay," I sighed, "start passing me piles and we'll start cleaning this out."

Carly grabbed a handful and dropped the items into my waiting arms. I didn't catch everything, but I walked the clothing to a nearby table already piled high with neatly folded T-shirts.

After I placed the fourth armload on the table, I heard Carly say, "What the heck?"

I turned and saw she had uncovered boxes. The sweaters and T-shirts had completely hidden three long, low boxes. Carly dug them out and passed them down to me.

On a hunch, she climbed down the ladder, rolled it to the next overstock curtain and pushed aside the jeans filling that space. There were more boxes. In the next 15 minutes, we recovered eight unopened boxes of various sizes. We called one of our fellow managers over and asked what we should do.

"Open them," Andy said. "It's probably just more from the holiday line that we forgot about. Get 'em out and mark them down. We need that stuff out of here before inventory."

Carly, box-cutting knife in hand, began slicing through the packing tape. Most of the boxes contained women's T-shirts, but two boxes held black and brown leather jackets, ones that were designed to look like jean jackets.

"When are these from?" Carly wondered. "How long have they been here?"

I pulled out a jacket, undoing the buttons to access the label that would tell me the date of the line.

"Fall zero zero," I read. "These are from last year. We should check the price."

We stacked the boxes on a rolling cart, pushing them to the cash registers at the front of the store. We had 12 styles of tees and two colours of leather jackets. As I handed Carly one style at a time to price check, she was uttering "Oh my God" and "Are you serious" over and over. I leaned over to see the price on the display. The T-shirts, originally $10, were now $0.97. Ninety-seven cents. There was a pause as Carly and I looked at each other, fully comprehending what a jackpot had landed in our hands. We were both grinning widely when I passed her the brown leather jacket.

"Are you ready?" she asked, her eyes shining with delight.

I felt like I had crested the climb on a roller coaster and was about to go hurtling down, laughing all the way. I nodded.

She scanned the ticket on the jacket. We stared at the number on the screen, blinking, unbelieving. The jackets, originally ticketed at $99, were now $1.97.

Carly was chuckling. I was digging through the box looking for my size.

"We should tell Andy," she paused. "Shouldn't we?"

We both hovered at the top of the hill, not wanting

to let go of the anticipation that came to us in the form of spectacular deals.

I clicked the microphone button of my headset and made the announcement to the ears of other associates and managers.

"We found some boxes of fall stock. Women's tees at 97 cents and leathers at a buck ninety-seven. We're at front cash if you want to claim some."

I anticipated a mad herd of people rushing up to see what we had. Instead, we had a trickle of staff come peer into the boxes, picking out a few items. Over my headset Andy said he wasn't interested.

"Price them and put them out," he said.

I had found the jacket in my size, both colours, and put them aside to purchase. Carly, on the other hand, was pulling tees out of the box by the armful.

"I'm buying them all," she said. "Sending them home."

"Home" was the Philippines. Carly intended to ship all the shirts to her family still living there.

On our way back to our hotel, Carly was giddy with excitement about the deals, as was I. We were both confused about the lack of interest from anyone else in the store. The next morning, when we were talking to one of the other merchandise managers, we discovered that the low prices were a novelty only to us. As Canadians, we are unaccustomed to seeing discounts that deep. In the US, however, it's common practice. What retailers lose on margins, they can make up in volume. In Canada, where the population of the entire country is less than the population of the state of California, it's a different story.

Later that year, when we were back in Canada, we were bombarded with half-zip fleece pullovers and I knew we were in trouble. The overstocks were overflowing. Our store manager had to go to Home Depot to buy shelving units that we built in the receiving area to handle the excess of the excess. We thought we were sent the units in error, but when my manager called head office, she was told the company was blitzing all stores across northern North America. It was a deliberate strategy cooked up by a buyer who grew up where the temperature rarely dips below 50 degrees Fahrenheit (or 10 degrees Celsius).

To corporate in San Francisco, this was no big deal. What they failed to understand was the difference in demographics and population as well. The number of people who came through our store in a week was equivalent to the number of customers who came through the store in Bloomington, Illinois, in one day. In downtown Chicago, that number of people had passed through the store's doors before lunchtime. There was no way we were going to be able to sell that much fleece, even at markdown prices.

Over the course of the entire fall and holiday season, there was fleece at every turn in every section. I already hated fleece before I started working at Old Navy. The static cling and the texture made me shudder. I could never get past the idea that fleece was actually plastic, made of the same material as pop bottles. It was warm, yes, but also sweaty. We were buried in fleece and we couldn't get rid of it. It was featured as the item of the week three times between September and December. The management team brainstormed contests to get our employees on the bandwagon. We even attempted to add phrasing at the cash register when someone was checking out. Our take was "Would you like fleece with that?" Even on markdowns, when most pieces were $9.99 or less, we still couldn't empty our displays, shelves, and overstock. Our store manager eventually had to beg corporate to allow us to ship back the fleece at the expense of our store's bottom line and management bonuses.

Once the store was fleece-free, one of my peers suggested we go out for drinks to celebrate. We toasted to "No more static cling!" "No more dry skin snagging the fabric!" and "No more plastic polyester!"

Our final toast was ribboned with bitterness. We had found out that the asshat at corporate who had made this horrible decision and over-ordered the fleece was promoted. Still, we raised our glasses, wishing him the best of luck, while wondering how we could make that next big step ourselves.

14

The Heiress

Hiring the right people is never easy, but when you have to hire enough people to staff a whole store, the task is enough to turn the most stoic of managers into a stammering maniac. Every management position I've held has required me to interview, train, and assess employees. By the time I was ready to leave Old Navy, I had participated in so much hiring and firing another company offered me a position in human resources.

I'm a terrible judge of character. I am easily swindled. A flirty smile, a crinkle at the eyes, a hint of shyness all appear to be desirable traits to me. If you tell me you're a hard worker who likes to get your hands dirty, I have no reason not to believe you. If you tell me this is the first job you've ever applied for, I'll be inspired to take you under my wing and show you the ropes. You can lie to my face about never being fired and I cannot see the lie. In short, I should never have been solely responsible for hiring anyone.

Fortunately, when I was part of Old Navy's management team, hiring for the 12 stores opening simultaneously in Ontario was a group sport. For six weeks, my fellow managers and I held group interviews. We asked pointedly designed questions such as, "How would it make you feel if a customer knocked over a display you just built?" At this stage of the interview process, we were assessing character. We were watching the group dynamic, looking for those who had trouble expressing themselves and letting the bullies identify themselves when they cut off other people mid-sentence. If they passed this early, analog social experiment and their resumé passed further scrutiny, they made it to the next round. In front of two managers, applicants were asked questions such as, "Tell me about a time you had a difficult customer." At the time, these types of situational questions weren't common. I loved them though. I may not be able to tell that you're lying about how long you worked at X store, but I know you're full of it if you can't tell me a single specific story about the shittiest customer you've ever dealt with. Spend a week in retail, and you'll have a story.

Despite this strategic line of questioning, I made some spectacularly poor hires. I hired the skinny teenager who bulked up by layering clothes at the end of every shift, then removing the stolen clothes when he was in his car. I caught him when I was on a smoke break and saw him flailing about in his small hatchback. Initially I thought the clothes flying around meant he was having sex in that car, until I counted four T-shirts coming off his back.

I hired the charismatic young man who didn't think we would check when he ticked the box on the application indicating he hadn't been hired by this company before. He had been, and he was fired with cause.

I hired the woman who was using marijuana daily for medicinal purposes two decades before she was legally permitted to do so.

I hired the mom who was re-entering the work force after raising her kids for 11 years, but spent an inordinate amount of time hiding in the stockroom because, she said, "Adults scare me."

It wasn't always a disaster though. I also hired an ambitious young woman who soaked up every bit of retail management knowledge I offered her and went on to management within the company. I hired a new immigrant from Russia who was a workhorse and ran the receiving department like an army general, a necessary attitude when you need to get 1,000 units ticketed, put on hangers, and on the floor in two hours. For non-retail folks, that's a feat akin to peeling 100 pounds of potatoes by hand before a pot of water boils. I took on an overqualified man fresh from earning his PhD in philosophy, but who had a wicked sense of humour and an astonishing knowledge about books from all genres.

And then there was Melanie. She had a tan, short, spiky hair, and was wearing very nice jewelry in her interview: a chunky gold necklace, a bright gold and diamond tennis bracelet, and diamond stud earrings. I was reluctant to offer this middle-aged woman a position when she first interviewed. One thing most retailers always ask for is full availability, meaning you need to be able to work anytime. It's a policy that never sat well with me. We needed students to work evenings and weekends and they were never available during the day. Why would we eliminate them from the hiring pool? Daytime workers have always been harder to find, and anyone who wanted a day shift was generally not willing to work evenings or weekends. Whenever I put forth a candidate with limited availability, I was instructed to remove them from the list. By the time Melanie's resumé was in front of me, indicating she was only looking for work during the day, I was so indoctrinated into this line of thinking that I initially discounted her before even meeting with her.

Her resumé wasn't spectacular. She had some experience working in retail, but the bulk of her working life was spent in administrative duties. There was a gap in her work history that I had come to know as the child-rearing-and-raising years. Our hiring fair was yielding many part-time employees, but full-time Monday to Friday staff were proving harder to find. It was this desperate need to fill gaps that earned Melanie an interview.

"I'm really looking for work that will keep me out of the house all day," she told me during her interview. "Ideally, I'd like to work from 8 a.m. to 3 p.m. That way I can get my kids off to school and be home when they're done."

I liked Melanie. She was up front about her needs and it was a refreshing change. Most interviewees have the same stock replies: "I love the brand," "I'm a hard worker," "I love working with the public." All lies, by the way. Brand love is code for "I'll steal for my friends." Hard worker translates into "I know how to look busy." Working with the public is another way to say "This is the only job I'm qualified for."

Melanie was frank when she shared that most of her retail experience came from being a shopper.

"I know almost everyone who will come through these doors," she said, smiling. "I've lived in this neighbourhood my whole life. I grew up with your customer base. I *am* your customer."

"Why do you think that's important?"

"I know these people. I know how they shop. I can manage them when they get… um… demanding."

"Have you considered applying for management?"

She shook her head so quickly her hair was jiggling on her head.

"God, no. I don't want any more responsibility other than showing up, doing my job well, and keeping the customers happy."

She certainly had the right attitude. She was also able to fill a slot that we had been having trouble filling.

"Would you be able to start earlier, say 7 a.m.?"

"I might be able to make that work, but I'd need some advance notice. Maybe a few days, if that's possible."

Schedules would be posted two weeks in advance, so that wouldn't be a problem. After consulting with the rest of my management team, we decided to forgo the rules about availability and hire her.

A few days into Melanie's training, one of my full-time direct reports in the baby section pulled me aside.

"I can't believe you hired Melanie," Frieda whispered.

My belly did a flip flop. Immediately, my mind went back to all the bad hires I had made in the past.

"I take it you know her?"

"Everyone in this neighbourhood knows her."

"I'm not surprised. She did say she grew up around here."

Frieda laughed. "That's a mild way to put it."

"What do you mean?" I tried not to furrow my brow, keeping my concern hidden.

"You know those buildings across the parking lot?"

There were three high-rise condominiums adjacent to the mall. They had been built 20 years earlier and were sold as luxury condos. The penthouses were all two-level suites.

"Melanie's father built those. And most of the developments north of the city. She inherited billions. And… she's an only child."

We both turned to look at Melanie, who was happily chatting with a customer paying for purchases at the cash register.

"Huh," was the only word I could summon.

Over time, I built up the nerve to ask Melanie about it.

"I heard you're an heiress," I said, not posing it as a question, but as a statement of fact.

"True," she grinned. "I told you everyone knows me around here."

"I have to ask the obvious question. Why are you working *here*?"

"I didn't want to run my father's company anymore. I quit."

My mouth hung open.

"Wait, you quit-quit or you sold the business?"

"I still own it," she shrugged, "but I hired someone else to run it. I had little kids. I wanted to stay home to raise them. I chose to bake cookies and cook dinner, not run out of the house every morning to make decisions about a business I didn't understand. Shopping and clothes... now *that* I understand."

Again, I was at a loss for words. "Huh."

Melanie turned out to be the most reliable employee I had. She was always on time, showed up with a smile, and took her role as the last person the customers see before they leave very seriously. She never once acted entitled. She emptied trash cans, peeled gum off the floor, and hung and folded clothes along with every other staff member.

It's a tricky game, hiring for retail, and that time I got it right.

15

The Pit of Retail Hell

I f you read Dante's *Divine Comedy* in high school or university and wondered whether it would ever be relevant, this chapter answers the question "Why would I ever need to know this in real life?"

The first part of Dante's *Divine Comedy*, the Inferno, describes Dante's journey through hell guided by Virgil. Hell is depicted as nine concentric circles of torment located within the Earth. It's the realm of punishment for terrible choices and abhorrent or illegal behaviour. Each circle is worse than the one that precedes it.

Working in clothing retail is akin to passing through all nine circles of Dante's hell. It can be an abyss of despair, a limbo for the working masses, a place where one can observe the worst in human behaviour. And, like Dante, you'll be wondering what you did deserve this punishment while simultaneously trying to find a way out. Except in retail, you don't have to claw your way past Satan. Just quit. There's always another job.

Here's the simplified form of Dana's Retail Inferno.

First Circle: Taking the job without knowing any better.

Second Circle: Being excited about using the employee discount before you realize most of your paycheque goes to clothing the company requires you to wear at work.

Third Circle: Watching the customers throw clothing around at the same time they're watching you fold it.

Fourth Circle: Dealing with management who wants you to work faster while simultaneously cutting back your hours.

Fifth Circle: Working at the cash register and handling returns.

Sixth Circle: Getting an annual performance review that sings your praises but doesn't give you a raise.

Seventh Circle: Going in to a job you hate every day and choking back the violence that threatens to explode from your body.

Eighth Circle: Taking spit in the face as a customer yells at you for not telling her silk is dry clean only.

Ninth Circle: The fitting rooms.

The treachery of the fitting rooms is a punishment of epic proportions. It's messy all the time. Clothes are strewn about and discarded like trash at the dump. I'm not proud to admit that as a manager I sent more than one employee to this purgatory in response to them being late, lazy, or rude.

Gross things happen behind closed doors. People leave dirty underwear and used sanitary pads on the floor. They won't think twice about having quick sex in there and leaving the used condom on top of the blue jeans, opened and leaking all over the denim. Someone will take the allotted 10 items in, and then shove the armful of rejected items and hangers into an employee's face without considering how rude this is. Or they just walk out on the mess, leaving all the clothes they tried on piled on the floor. During the big sales, the fitting room is a revolving door of frustration and overwhelm. One year, the two employees running our fitting room were so overtaken by rejected clothing they had to lock off a room and pile everything inside. That night, when I opened the door, it was an apocalyptic explosion, a tangle of arms, legs, torsos, and necks without bodies. It took five of us three hours to re-hang, re-fold, and put everything back. It was so bad, I still have recurring PTSD nightmares about that day, even after 20 years. I'll startle awake, thinking I'm buried under the clothes, slowly suffocating.

Recovery—the process of sorting, reshelving, or destroying all the rejected items—happens all the time all over the store. In a grocery store, recovery includes employees walking the aisles, usually close to closing time, collecting the misplaced items from the shelves. This could be a can of tomato soup sitting in among the chocolate bars, a reversal in choice that I completely understand. It might be a bunch of dill nestled in among the dish soap. Woe to the recovery team who finds a pint of ice cream dumped among the boxes of pasta and now has to clean up the melted mess. At the bookstore, recovery meant reshelving books people had left on the tables and chairs scattered around the store.

In housewares, the endless folding of towels was the biggest chore, but there were also pots and pans to re-shelve, sheets to repackage, and small appliances to put back into the boxes.

But in clothing retail, recovery is a lesson in human behaviour. Customers have no qualms about pulling apart a shelf of folded shirts, refusing your offer of assistance while being completely oblivious that you're demonstrating your sharp reflexes, catching the items being knocked off the shelves before they hit the floor. You have to stand by idly, smiling (but with murder in your eyes) as a customer throws items in your face, raging about price, size, or quality. And then you have to clean up that mess. I have had to watch from the sidelines as a group of drunk college boys amuse them-selves by moving baby clothing to the men's section and trying on women's clothes as they get in touch with their feminine sides. When they get bored and leave, I have three sections to re-merchandise.

Clothing retail, by its very nature, will prepare you for the worst of humankind. When you get out, you'll have life skills that will help you navigate the toughest of circumstances. You'll be able to calm the bullies, control your own impulses, and navigate any emotional breakdowns. But above all, you will never, ever, as long as you live, drop an item of clothing on the floor or leave clothes in a heap in the fitting room. You'll be a better customer for all humankind.

16

Liquid Lunch

With tens of thousands of stores in more than 3,700 malls in Canada, it surprised me just how small the retail management world could be. As I moved through companies, I encountered regional managers I had worked with before. At an annual general meeting, I ran in to a district manager I had worked with at a different company. On more than one occasion, I'd walk into an interview in progress to find the interviewee was someone I had fired. Gossip was never more than a phone call away. When your spouse also works in retail, as my first husband did, the world gets even smaller. You need to be careful about how you conduct yourself because your reputation will follow you to every store.

I had a reputation as a driven, customer-centric, and creative merchandiser. I took chances with displays, broke protocol with how things were normally done, and tended to ignore the planograms because I knew what my customers wanted—and what they wanted should always be at eye level. I inspired my employees to be creative, to drop everything to help a customer, and to find a way to laugh every shift.

Despite what I thought were stellar qualities, especially in leadership, I was also known to be bold, a person who spoke her mind, who pushed back against rules that didn't make sense. In hindsight, I'm not sure why anyone wanted to hire me at all.

At almost every company, I got in trouble repeatedly: for taking a publisher's sales representative out for lunch (on my dime) so I could secure enough best-selling books for the holiday season; for spending 45 minutes with a customer who came in looking for new knives and left with everything she would need to outfit her newly renovated kitchen; for climbing a ladder to the overstock to find a size for a customer instead of finding an employee to do it.

"Your job is to manage the people, Dana, not climb on ladders."

My GM didn't agree with me when I said the customer would not understand why I walked away to find someone to help her when I was standing directly in front of the item she wanted. Every day in retail management is filled with stupidity like this.

Rules for staff seem to apply only to some people and not to others. I considered myself a rule follower, but with flexibility. As a smoker, I had to feed my habit on non-sanctioned smoke breaks throughout my shift. My non-smoking colleagues were always bothered by this, but in my mind, I was skipping my scheduled breaks, using my time to grab a few puffs here and there, and that was okay. My bosses were similarly annoyed and I was once written up for "endangering employees and putting the inventory at risk" for having a smoke outside the loading dock at 6:30 a.m. I stood on the metal stairs adjacent to the dock, the back door propped open and every employee knew where I was if they needed to find me. While I was unconcerned about not being inside the building when the store was closed, my district and general managers at this particular company held a different view.

"If you are not inside the store and something happens, we're liable for any injures that might occur," I was told in my disciplinary meeting.

"Aren't we liable even if we're all in the store?" I asked.

At this point in my career, I had worked in several stores with many different companies. I was becoming less tolerant of what I viewed as utter bullshit in this industry.

"That's beside the point," my boss answered. "The code of conduct stipulates that there must be a manager in the store at all times."

I shook my head.

"That's not what it says. It says, and I'm para-phrasing here, 'managers on duty are to be accessible to associates and customers at all times.' Everyone knows where I am when I'm smoking."

The general manager was flipping pages in the oper-ations manual binder resting on her legs. The district manager was scanning the forms on the desk, papers that would go into my personnel file. They were a united front. Even if I was right, they would not acknowledge it.

"Please take only your scheduled breaks," my general manger advised me. When I refused to sign off on the disciplinary notice, the meeting was over and I went back to the store to finish my day.

"It's a miracle you weren't fired on the spot," my husband admonished me at dinner. "Insubordination is cause, you know."

"Aren't you supposed to be on my side?" I knew he wouldn't be. He was a company man, despite the fact that we weren't even working for the same company.

"What are you going to do if you get fired?" he said, ignoring my question.

"Then I'll find another job. It's not like there is a shortage of retail management jobs."

Two months later we would have a similar conversation when I was written up for taking too long to eat an apple.

"Apparently one of the other managers complained about it. It feels like they're looking for ammunition to fire me," I grumbled.

"How long did you take?" he responded.

It stunned me that he couldn't see how ridiculous it was to be written up for eating. I never complained about the extra hours I put in when people from head office paid a surprise visit and asked me to walk the store with them as they dispensed merchandising directives.

In retail, give and take is unbalanced. Middle

managers are expected to give even when upper management has been unreasonable in the take.

After the apple fiasco, I started paying very close attention to what my colleagues were doing. I had my suspicions about who might have filed the complaint.

One of the managers I had worked with from the beginning was forever watching the clock. Malik was, pardon my language, a slimy fucker. He kissed ass. Was spineless when it came to making decisions. When faced with a difficult customer, he would shrug his shoulders, telling the customer he was following company policy and his hands were tied. He back-stabbed other managers and the employees. He thought nothing of throwing an associate under the bus for his own personal and professional gain. It's an understate-ment to say Malik and I did not get along.

I made mental notes of his own infractions: multiple personal phone calls, not answering pages when summoned as the manager-on-duty for the shift, walking around with unfolded shirts and pants tossed over his shoulder so he could look busy. I observed him for two days, and at the same time I was second-guessing my every interaction, being less than the friendly person I was normally. I gobbled my food while watching the clock and took only my scheduled breaks to avoid being reprimanded again. I was suspi-cious of everyone, untrusting, fearful that every deci-sion I made would be questioned and twisted into cause for my dismissal. But I really didn't like the anxious, mean person I was becoming.

Then, when a new manager came on, my paranoia

kicked into high gear. I thought Emma was hired to replace me, and I never gave her a chance. I disliked her from the first day, based solely on my own insecurity. When Malik was asked to train her, I viewed that as his reward for being a snitch.

"Are you okay?" Frieda, my full-time direct report, had picked up on the change in my behaviour. She was twice my age, with way more people experience. I always treated her with respect, asking her for help and soliciting her ideas. She had remarkable patience, the kind that comes from drifting in and out of the retail world. She'd been working in retail in some capacity—from sales associate to management to administration—for more than 30 years. She wasn't exactly a lifer, though. She had taken time off to raise her kids. She stepped out of the workforce again when her father fell ill. She had never gone to university and tried any job that came her way.

"I was not built to make coffee and smile pretty," she once told me. I laughed harder than I should have because Frieda was almost six feet tall with crooked teeth and eyes that were too close together. She was amazing with the customers, engaging them in long conversations. I once witnessed a customer crying and hugging Frieda after she helped her find a baby gift that fit her budget but looked like she had spent more than she did. Frieda was so good at reading people and carried an aura of trust. She could have been a therapist.

"You're different these days. Smiling less."

"I'm fine," I assured her. I desperately wanted to

vent, but even after almost two years of working together, that was a line I could not cross.

"There's something about her I don't like," she said quietly, following my eyes to Malik and Emma. "I just can't put my finger on it."

I couldn't agree with her, not publicly. In my head, though, I was glad for the validation that it wasn't just paranoia and insecurity fuelling my thoughts.

Since Malik was training Emma, their schedules were identical for two months. They took the same breaks and went out for lunch at the same time. When Emma's training was complete and she was taking on her own shifts, she still reached out only to Malik. She called him on his days off instead of asking one of the other three sales or merchandising managers in the store for help. It was weird and everyone noticed. Employees were gossiping about them, saying they were drinking at lunch and spending a lot of time in the stockroom. The other managers, myself included, subconsciously distanced ourselves from this odd couple. They were team players on a team of two. The whole vibe in the store was off-kilter, but nobody knew what to do about it.

Because of my history of being written up, I became ridiculously conscious of time, not just mine, but others' as well. I stuck to the schedule, only leaving the sales floor when it was time for my break. It was this diligence that made me notice when others, specifically Malik and Emma, were not *where* they were supposed to be *when* they were supposed to be there. Malik and Emma would vanish for lunch, sometimes for hours.

On more than one occasion, when my lunch was supposed to follow theirs, I was left waiting for more than an hour past their scheduled return.

I took notes, recording times and dates. I confronted them, telling them they needed to watch the clock and come back on time. Malik thanked me for being diligent and said they both hadn't realized they'd been gone so long. I wanted to report them, but with my own history, I was reluctant to draw any attention to myself.

"Just do your own job and never mind what they're doing," my husband advised me.

But I couldn't help myself. Rage built inside me. I fumed about being reprimanded for eating an apple while these two went missing from the store for more than two hours, at least once per week. How was it that I was the only manager who noticed?

I rebelled in the only way I knew how: I resumed my smoke breaks. I was more careful about it this time. I had employees I could trust who would come get me if I was needed. I found a perfect place to hide: out on the loading dock and around the corner from the front doors, facing the part of the parking lot that was rarely used. Every mall has a section of a parking lot like this. It's not near any entry doors, sometimes it's adjacent to the dumpsters, and it's usually the dumping ground for all kinds of crap piled up around the donation bins. I could stand there and smoke, my headset still on my head. I was close enough for the radio to still work, but far enough away that I could enjoy my cigarette in peace.

On one of these breaks, when again Emma and

Malik were MIA, I stood out there in the height of summer, tucked beside the garbage bin enclosure, stealing a bit of shade and ignoring the stink. There were few cars in the lot. I watched a car pull into a spot, then watched the two people inside put their heads close together. At first, I thought they were deep in conversation, but it soon became clear they weren't in a whispered conspiracy. They were very clearly making out. I felt embarrassed, then giddy, then sad. I didn't want to be caught watching, but here were two young lovers sharing a moment, a passion that was missing from my own marriage.

When they emerged from the car, a small squeak passed my lips. I dropped my cigarette and ground it under my shoe. I was frozen to the spot, trying to be even more invisible. Malik and Emma met at the hood of the car, he, leaning against it, she, leaning against him between his legs. They kissed and I was close enough to see Malik nibble on Emma's bottom lip. He was married. She had a boyfriend. I smiled, not because there was heartbreak on the horizon for their partners, but because management who were *together* together, could NOT work in the same store.

Hell, yes, I was going to report this. I should have let the story play out on its own, but I was an angry and petty 20-something who had her chance to deliver some karma.

"You can't snitch without getting yourself in trouble," my soon-to-be-ex pointed out. "Just leave it alone."

"Leave it alone?" I said with disbelief. "I can't leave

it alone. I get written up for eating an apple, but they can get away with two-hour liquid lunches?"

"Wait," he said, knitting his brows together, "they're getting drunk too?"

I rolled my eyes. "Not that kind of liquid…"

It took him longer than it should have to figure it out. Daft jackass.

So, like a petulant child, I told my store manager what I had seen. In an atmosphere of distrust and paranoia, I knowingly put my neck on the line. I reported what I saw. Malik and Emma were pulled in for a meeting. They admitted they were involved. They apologized for taking longer lunches and asked to be reassigned to different stores. Neither were fired for their long, sex-filled lunch hours.

I, on the other hand, was written up for taking an unapproved break. It was the last time that happened. That evening, I began the search for another job. Greener pastures. I learned a valuable lesson about retail: there are people who do what they want and get away with it and there are people who are targets.

You know that Maya Angelou quote about "When people show you who they are, believe them"? The same rule applies for a company. How they treat a person from their first interview or their first day is all you need to know.

17

Girl, Out of Body

Merchandising done well is invisible to the consumer. It's an interesting contradiction. With the right manipulation of elements, visuals can tell a story and stir the feeling of "I want that." An eye-catching display of perfectly folded and symmetrical jeans or a well-dressed mannequin are both effective ways to change want into need. Merchandising is designed to be a feast for our eyes and a trigger of desire for our brain. It's meant to reduce the number of decisions we have to make when we're in a store.

If the idea of digging through discount bins at a warehouse sale causes you anxiety, you're the perfect candidate for some slick merchandising. I am one of those people. I'll pay a little more to walk up to shelves stocked with flat irons rather than sink my hands into a 72-litre tote filled with socks, mugs, backpacks, and spatulas with the hope that a flat iron is somewhere in there. There's a reason the Amazon returns store (seriously, Google that) charges $10 or less for an item it sells online for much more. Liquidators are not known for their merchandising skills. It's 100% a dump-and-run situation.

Merchandising in its most basic form simply means presenting goods in a store with the goal of selling them. But that only scratches the surface of what's actually a really complex mix of human psychology and clip-strips. Window displays aren't merely advertising space, they are carefully designed to entice people into the store. Merchandising is an elaborate sport involving colour, lighting, placement, and storytelling. And before it was taught in vocational schools, you had to be born a merchandiser. It was an artistic and elite group, but without the creepy secret clubs and the money. Hang on. This is retail, so yes to the secret clubs.

I dipped my toe into merchandising at my first retail management job at Chapters. At the time, I didn't have a name or skill attached to what I was doing. When the literary prize season kicked off, it made sense to me to build a display of books that were nominated for the Giller, Pulitzer, or Booker. The same held true for the Academy Award nominations. When people were talking about movies, I built a table filled with novels that were made into films. It was a bonus if one of those had been adapted into a nominated film that year.

Books are not as easy to merchandise as one might think. Too many books on a table is chaos; too few has zero impact. My tables had depth: the display was a deliberate mix of books on stands so you could see their gorgeous covers, books laid flat and cascading from a high pile to a low one, and books whose spines were eye-catching, especially when five copies of the same title were grouped, like a perfect formation of soldiers. I used end caps (the space at the front end of an aisle) to display romance novels with red covers for February or art books with blue covers during October to commemorate Picasso's birthday.

My creative and business brain was triggered on a daily basis. I had a planner where I jotted down my ideas for monthly displays. An "Oscar-winning musical movies derived from books" display morphed into a display of children's books about wizards. My stream of consciousness during that summer and fall went from *The Wizard of Oz* (Best Picture, 1940) to Terry Pratchett's *Discworld* series (UK's bestselling author of the 1990s), to the newly released *Harry Potter and the Philosopher's Stone*. I still remember the weekend I took home that quirky little book about the boy wizard and curled up in my oversized reading chair smoking cigarettes, unable to stop turning the pages.

Back then, I had full control of what books were in the sections I managed. I could place orders for what I thought would interest our customers. Demographics mattered and what readers wanted in a mall in a posh neighbourhood was sometimes very different than what would sell in a larger, more culturally diverse area. Bargain books were distributed to stores automatically and when 50 books about Judaism arrived in my store in St. Catharines—a small city with a Jewish population of less than 500—I laughed out loud. I knew I would sell maybe five to 10 copies. I got on the phone and called a colleague at a store in a predominantly

Jewish neighbourhood in Toronto and she was thrilled to take my excess. Automated distribution had sent her three copies.

"Do you have any Haynes manuals you can't move?" I asked her.

"I haven't sold a single one," she snorted through the phone.

Haynes manuals were the go-to source for do-it-yourself mechanics. Any car, any model, any year—there was a manual for that. In St. Catharines, where the GM plant was the largest employer, these were a popular item. In a neighbourhood where most people would never look under the hood of their cars unless they needed windshield washer fluid, these manuals would never move.

"How many do you have?"

I waited while she checked her inventory.

"I have 32 copies, various models. Want 'em?"

"Yes, please."

In my mind, I was already building the end cap display. When the books arrived, I flipped through the generic signage we had in the store, looking for one that would work. I found "Manuals" and "DIY," but if I wanted something clever, I would have to order it. I mulled over a few ideas and landed on "Spend Time, Save Money." Corny, but appropriate. I put 14 manuals on display and had to fill the holes over the coming weeks. Not every manual sold, but I learned that part of merchandising was showing people things they didn't know existed and planting the bug in their brains that this was something they needed.

Not all my merchandising was brilliant. I stacked jeans so high they toppled like dominoes the second someone tried to pull out a size. I hung shoes on hooks, which looked really edgy until someone tried to reach for a pair hung high and was showered in a cascade of footwear. I repeated that stupidity with socks.

To be successful as a merchandiser, I had to be creative, but I didn't have to be an artist. I could see the potential of mixing stripes with dots, of layering textures and grouping complementary colours. I aimed to catch the shopper's eye and generate interest. I learned to read a planogram, a carefully designed visual map of what goes where, what gets hung, and what needs to be folded. As a creative, this adherence to structure was not always fun and sometimes quite boring. On occasion, I was given opportunities to wave my merchandising flag and create displays that went against corporate direction. I knew when to fight and when to acquiesce. When the merchandising team from head office swept into my store and tut-tutted over my decision to use binder clips to hang an entire outfit from one hanger, I explained why I did it. My customers in that particular store liked to have a whole package put together before their eyes—top, bottom, and accessories. My goal, I explained to the suits, was to have the customer point and say, "I want that" and buy all the pieces. If they came in looking for a baby gift on a budget, I wanted them to see the potential of spending a few more bucks. If they came in looking for a new pair of jeans, I wanted them to walk out with a sweater, a down vest, and a scarf. In retail, everything is measured, including the number of units per transaction.

I was often criticized for the risks I took, but a new-to-the-company director of merchandising saw potential in what I was trying to do. He took some photos of my displays in the baby section, nodded, and smiled at me while I stood off to the side, my lunch gurgling uneasily in my stomach. In retail, you never know which way a head office walkthrough will go. On more than one occasion, I was expecting praise, but was instead written up for some ridiculous infraction. By this point in my career, I knew to shut my mouth and hope for the best.

"Do you think he's taking photos for evidence when they fire me?" I whispered to my colleague Frieda.

"They'd be crazy to do that," she said out of the side of her mouth.

"I know you've seen people sacked for less," I said.

"And I've seen people promoted for doing worse."

When the walkthrough was done and our store manager left with the head office crew to go out for lunch, the tension in my neck eased off. I could worry about what was happening, or might happen, or where I would find my next job, or I could resume the project Frieda and I were working on. I opted to hang baby clothes.

A little more than two months later, we were notified that the director of merchandising was once again going to visit our store. The evening before the visit, all the managers were in the store, cleaning and perfecting and checking the planograms to ensure our displays matched corporate direction. Every store I ever worked in, it was the same story. We'd let things slide until corporate came to visit. Clothing retail was the worst. The night before the visit, we—meaning management— were working late into the night, folding and cleaning and organizing by size. After a few hours' sleep, we were back in the store, dusting, mopping, and checking the inventory to make sure everything was perfect. It was exhausting.

"Wouldn't it be better to let them see how things really are?" I once asked.

The way the team fell silent, you'd think I had proposed burning the store to the ground. The sound of the floor waxers somewhere in the mall drifted through the metal rolling gate that closed off the front of the store.

"What?" I pushed. "Why should we scramble like this? Why are we hiding the fact that we don't have enough sparkle star T-shirts to fill the display?"

"They don't care about what's wrong," my store manager explained, "they only want to see that we're doing things right."

"Even if that means we have four shirts hanging on an arm when there should be 15? Why wouldn't we tell them we're having stock issues? Wouldn't they want to know that?"

She shook her head. "If it was the operations team coming, then sure, we could tell them about that. This is the *merchandising* team. They don't care about logistics and distribution. They care about how things look."

I opened my mouth to continue the argument, but

caught a subtle head shake from one of my fellow managers. Linda had been a merchandiser for almost a decade at a major department store. She was an ally, but in a very quiet way. She followed the rules, yet always had a sympathetic ear for my complaints, often advising me to pick my battles. If she was signalling me to stop, I needed to stop.

The entire management team was on the sales floor, trying to look busy while we waited for the people from head office. Typical of these kinds of visits, the window was more vague than an internet installation appointment. *In the morning*, was the only information we had. So we waited, turning our heads each time bodies entered our field of vision, like meerkats in the desert landscape. I was torn between wanting to dive in and make some changes to my department and the dread of being caught with my section in mid-display. If I started moving clothes around, I could very well be caught with my pants down. So instead of jumping in and building, Frieda and I drew out the plan for what we would do once the walk was over. As the merchandise manager for kids and babies, I would be the last department to be walked. It could be hours before Frieda and I could get things done. Naturally, in the landscape of poor timing common in retail, this walk was happening the day before a major seasonal change in my department. I mentally prepared myself for a long day and night. The changes would have to be made before we opened the store the next morning. This was another thorn in my side that I wanted to vocalize, but couldn't. Instead, I let Frieda vent to me.

"Why would they do this walk the day before we have to change everything. Shouldn't they come after?"

I shrugged my shoulders without pulling my eyes off the detailed reports telling me exactly what product had arrived for my displays.

"I know, I know. You can't change these things," she sighed. "I can stay late if you need me to." This is one reason why I loved Frieda. She was all in, all the time. She cared as much about the customers as I did. She was excited about new product and she enjoyed creating eye-catching displays.

Shortly after 11 a.m., the merchandising team walked into the store. For the next hour and a half, they walked men's and women's. At 12:30 p.m., they announced they were going to lunch, taking the store manager and the other two department managers with them.

"Would you mind watching the store alone until then?" one of the head office people asked me. "We'll do the walk in kids and babies when we return."

I smiled and nodded. I didn't have a choice. I was tired and hungry and now feeling like I was under-valued because no one was going to buy *me* lunch. I was being picked last for the gym team.

"Go into receiving and eat there," Frieda said, standing behind me, also watching them all walk away.

"You need to take your lunch, too," I said. "You go and then I'll try to grab a bite before they come back." My stomach was crushing itself with hunger and the edge of a headache was starting to build in my fore-head. Thirty minutes later, Frieda emerged from the lunchroom, shoving a power bar she bought from the vending machine into my hand.

"Go, now," she ordered, like a mother who wasn't going to take any crap.

I laughed as I headed to the receiving area, tearing open the wrapper and taking a bite as I used my ass to push open the swinging doors.

It was quiet back there, the receiving crew having gone home for the day. It was just me, broken-down boxes, and rolling racks of clothes waiting to be put out once the walkthrough was over. It was peaceful here, dimly lit with the vague smell of seawater, clothing dye, and plastic. It was the smell of Made in Asia.

I wolfed down the power bar in four bites, fully conscious of the trouble I would be in if I wasn't on the sales floor when everyone came back. I had oat bits stuck in my teeth, so I dashed to the bathroom to rinse my mouth. I had to pee, too, and I stood in front of a stall contemplating whether I had time to empty my bladder. Finding yourself having to measure the fallout from being written up versus a urinary tract infection is a sad place to be.

It was past two o'clock when the team returned from lunch. They went into the management office without even acknowledging me. No one came to relieve me so I could have some lunch. Another hour passed. Then another.

"What a bunch of assholes," Frieda muttered on her way out the door at the end of her shift. "You deserve better."

After a long night and an even longer day, I was

grateful for her kindness. I was tired and stressed out, but at least the power bar managed to keep my hunger at bay. As I waited for my turn with the merchandising team, I vacillated between being pissed off enough to want to find a new job and putting on a happy face as I filled in the part-timers who were coming in for their shifts.

"Focus on keeping things neat and tidy. If a customer picks up a shirt, you need to be refolding it before it hits the table," I advised them.

Shortly before 5 p.m., the director of merchandising strolled into the baby section. I was resizing the baby jeans hanging on a post, putting them back in order from size 0–3 months up to 5T.

"Dana, we want to test these new merchandising hangers in kids and babies," he said, handing me a flat head. The top half of the hanger was made of medium density fibreboard, commonly called MDF. It featured a smiling girl with short blond hair painted just below her ears. She had a neck and bare shoulders. Where her torso should have been, a rectangular wire filled the space with clips at the bottom. A wire loop was stuck to the back of her head.

"You'll put these at the front of the display arm," he showed me, pulling off a pair of jeans I had just hung. "That's what the loop on the back is for. The whole piece is meant to enable you to display a complete outfit together."

"Oh, like I was doing the last time you were here," I smiled. I was lit up inside. My idea had made it to head office. This was the stepping stone I had been waiting for! My time had come to get off the sales floor and become part of the national merchandising team. Next stop after that: head office in San Francisco.

"Yes. That was a great idea. You inspired me to add the head and shoulders. Makes it more friendly and appealing. I've left a bunch of these in the office for you. Boys and girls and babies. The new planogram will be sent out via courier tomorrow. Thanks. Nice to see you."

He left the store, joining the rest of his team who were waiting out front. From the back of the store, where my section was, I had an unobstructed view to the mall. I watched them for a minute, laughing and pointing and checking their watches. I stood there, a disembodied girl in my hands, feeling like I'd been slapped in the face. There was not going to be any promotion. He had just given me all the recognition I was going to get. My idea was going to be applied in every store in North America and someone else was going to take all the credit.

I swallowed my heartbreak and shuffled to the back office. I needed a break. I wanted to get out of the store, smoke a million cigarettes, and eat a giant bag of chips. I played out what I could say that was passive aggressive, letting my store manager know I was pissed off about so many things. I still had the head in my hands.

"Oh, hey," she said when I walked into the office. "I'm glad you're here. Those boxes are for you." She tilted her chin to a half dozen boxes piled in a corner.

"Can you get those out of here and make a space for

them in receiving?" She turned her back on me, busying herself with something at the computer.

My stomach bubbled. I started grinding my teeth. I had a moment of glee as I imagined myself twisting her head off her neck and planting it atop one of the new display hangers.

Instead, all I could manage was a quiet and meek "Sure."

"Wait," she said as I navigated pulling open the door with an awkward box in my arms. "Did you get lunch today?"

It was 6 p.m. I had been in the store for 12 hours.

"No."

"Take dinner now. But can you be back in 20 minutes? I have some paperwork to finish before closing and I need you on the floor."

The other three managers had already gone home for the day. I spent the rest of the night wondering when I had become so invisible, and so devalued. I questioned why I tolerated it and how I let myself be treated as less than a human being. Instead of quitting on the spot, which I really wanted to do, I went home and lay down on my couch, trying to figure out how I could do better and contribute even more to the store. I fell asleep fully clothed and dreamed of disembodied babies chasing me with blue jeans clipped below their shoulders.

My inability to just accept the divisions of power in retail was part of my issue and an attitude that stunted my career progress. I always thought we were on the same team, aiming for the same target. Making shopping a positive experience, generating sales, and keeping our good employees seemed like reasonable goals. I was wrong. No matter which company I worked for, the rules were pretty much the same:

- Do as head office tells you.
- Keep your opinions to yourself.
- Take the blame for slack sales.
- Do more with less.

While I didn't fight these rules, I questioned them. I had the audacity to tell head office that it was impossible for two people in receiving to unpack, label, and hang 2,000 pieces of clothing in three hours. I pointed out that we couldn't sell what we didn't have. I built displays using my own imagination when product that head office wanted us to display sold out, wasn't replenished, or never came into the store in the first place. I knew, but didn't want to acknowledge, that every time I opened my mouth, I was probably committing career suicide.

18

Telling a Story, Selling a Garlic Press

"How would you merchandise towels?"

The question caught me completely off-guard. Until my interviewer lobbed that one at me, I was nailing all the typical questions: *Tell me about a time you had to fire an employee, tell me about the last time you handled a difficult customer,* and *tell me about a time you disagreed with your manager.*

"I wouldn't," I answered after taking 10 seconds to think about it.

"Why not?"

"Beyond sorting the towels by colour and size, what more needs to be done? People don't come in looking for ideas on how to make their linen closets more appealing. They need blue bath towels, or pretty hand towels that complement the wallpaper in their powder room. I would make it easy for customers to find what they need by keeping things neat and orderly."

The human resources woman interviewing me for a sales manager role at HomeSense was hard to read. She hadn't nodded her head or smiled at all whenever I gave an answer. When we were done, I walked away vacillating between feeling like I had nailed the interview and wondering what I could have done better.

When she called me a week later to offer me the job, I was surprised and extremely thrilled. I was ready to leave Old Navy and move on with my career. HomeSense was owned by TJX, the company behind T.J. Maxx, Marshalls, and HomeGoods. To my ambitious mind, there was more opportunity for growth and promotion. All I had to do was shine.

While I was getting a handle on selling discounted housewares, I was also building my skills as a merchandiser. Part of my job was putting together vignettes on the end caps—the space at the front end of every merchandising fixture. Walk into any store that has this kind of set-up and you'll find great merchandising on the front and clearance garbage on the end. Every store I've ever been in, from drugstores to high-end department stores, uses these spaces the same way, hiding the odds and ends, stuff that was found in the stockroom from two Christmases past, things that don't sell, and items on the verge of expiry. Clearance is always buried in the back, jammed into racks and onto shelves, discarded, but holding onto hope, like the clothes you anticipate will fit again one day.

All the money, energy, and creativity of the merchandiser is focused on the front. Vendors pay a lot of money to have their products featured on the high-traffic end caps in some stores because they bring the items into focus for the consumer.

At HomeSense, there were no vendors vying for those coveted spots. As the merchandising manager, my job was to make every end cap in the store tell a story and to move goods while doing so. It was entirely up to me and my staff to determine what items to place and how to display them. Usually, the end cap displays were dependant on what merchandise we had a lot of and had to move, any emerging trends that were spilling into housewares, such as popular new colours, and what my team thought was pretty.

Building end caps and displays was like solving a cryptic crossword and I've been a puzzle lover since I was a kid. I had more items than space, and that meant I had to get creative with my allotted three shelves. I had to nest items, use risers (plastic, upside down U-shaped pieces that acted as a shelf), and use items for purposes other than what they were meant for. I once used a short, wide-mouthed vase filled with blue glass beads to display orange enamelled garlic presses. Kitchen utensils are always the hardest to display. The choices have always been to hang them or bin them, neither of which gets anyone excited about a whisk. I stuck the arms into the beads with the heads sticking out like flowers facing the sun. I had 15 of the garlic presses to move and I thought it was a clever way to sell them. One of my full-timers, Suzanne, a brilliant merchandiser, laughed at me when I put the vase on the top shelf of the end unit.

"Seriously? Garlic presses?" she smiled.

"Why not? I think it looks pretty."

"That's a recipe for disaster."

I looked at the vibrant splash of colour and then back at her. "How so?"

"I'll let you think about it," she grinned, then walked away to work on a display of Portmeirion porcelain. She had the easy job today. The floral dinnerware, tea sets, and placemats always sold themselves no matter how we displayed them.

I stood back, examining the vase. I couldn't see anything wrong with what I had done. I walked down the aisle, looking for other items to build the display. This was one of the parts of my job I enjoyed the most. I was in control of telling a story with product. Would I make this a utensil display? Would I tell the story of garlic with sauté pans and a selection of packaged foods containing garlic? Should I create a spice cabinet with a variety of spices, kitchen garlands of ceramic peppers and garlic, and microplanes, mortar and pestles, and electric grinders?

I was collecting tea towels when I heard a crash coming from the end of the aisle. I ran to the source and found a woman frozen in front of the end cap, her face turning crimson, an orange garlic press clenched in her hand.

"I'm... I'm sorry. I just pulled this out and the whole thing just... fell."

In my peripheral vision, I saw Suzanne wink and point a finger gun at me.

"Don't worry about it," I assured the woman. "These things happen. You didn't get cut, did you?"

Please say no. Even the smallest cut requires a mountain of paperwork for an incident report.

The woman looked at her hands and arms and confirmed she was unharmed. Inside, I sighed with relief.

"I'm sorry about the vase. I'll gladly pay for that."

I shook my head. "No need. Don't worry about it at all."

When the woman put the garlic press back on the shelf among the shards of glass and walked away, Suzanne let her laughter erupt.

"Told ya," she snickered.

For a moment, I thought I should make her clean up the mess. My ego was bruised and my employee was laughing at me. She could have been clear and warned me ahead of time of what she foresaw. Instead, she chose to be coy and play a game. This was not how you moved ahead in retail. If she had any aspirations of moving into management, she would need to step up and contribute in a valuable way. And not ridicule her boss. Obviously, I would have to coach her on how to tactfully make helpful suggestions without seeming like she was stepping on toes. While it would be within my managerial duties to delegate the clean-up to an employee, that wasn't the kind of manager I was. I subscribed to two mantras, both of which were contradictions of what is normally acceptable in retail management:

1. Never ask an employee to do anything you wouldn't be willing to do yourself.
2. If you caused the problem, you find the solution.

In the corporate world, those two concepts work brilliantly. It's how you lead, inspire, and empower a team. There are very few retail managers, especially at the head office level, who subscribe to that line of thinking. It takes a special kind of manager to say, "Hey, Dana, can you help me clear the clogged toilets in the women's bathroom?" and dive in to the task together. I've only ever had one manager who stepped in the shit with and for the staff. I learned from her and modelled my management style after everything she taught me.

"Suzanne, can you stand here until I come back with a broom and a dustpan?"

As I swept up the mess, Suzanne went to get one of the large, black garbage cans we kept in the back. When I was called to the front for an authorization signature on a void, I asked Suzanne to keep the customers away from the mess. By the time I got back to the end cap, the mess was cleaned, the garbage can was back in the stockroom, and Suzanne was building a Turkish world of spices, samovars, and cone-shaped, elaborately painted tagines. She added decorative mosaic tiles and mosaic candle holders, as well as an array of hand-painted ceramic bowls of varying sizes. It was an inviting explosion of colour. It was beyond gorgeous. On the middle shelf, Suzanne had placed a hammered metal tea pot. I had no idea where she found it, but the slightly blueish hue of the metal was the perfect complement and display for 15 orange enamelled garlic presses.

19

The Designers

I've lined up for shopping only three times in my life: when The Gap opened their first store in Ontario, when lululemon had a massive warehouse sale, and when my current husband Jeff and I went to purchase a much-needed new television at Best Buy on Boxing Day. That Boxing Day lineup was the one that convinced me to never line up for anything again, if I could help it. We stood sixth in line, huddled into our winter coats, shivering from the bitter cold. We faced the wall, hiding our faces from the wind-driven snow. It took almost an hour before either one of us clued in to the idea of leaving our car running so we could alternate standing in line and sitting in the warm car.

"Next time we should bring a couple thermoses of coffee," I said to my husband as I relieved him in line.

"No," he said as he walked away. "There will not be a next time."

He was right. For me, this experience was not repeated. But being the wonderful man he is, Jeff did stand in line for another Boxing Day sale years later when we needed to replace a television after one of our children launched a Wii remote into the screen during a passionate game of bowling.

Working as a manager at HomeSense, I never anticipated seeing a lineup outside the store, but every Tuesday, if I was working the opening shift, a line would start forming around 8:30 a.m. and build for the next hour. These were the designers, the interior decorators, and the home stagers coming to see what came in fresh off the truck. Somehow, with remarkable acuity, they had figured out that our truck arrived on Monday and the freshest items were on the sales floor by opening on Tuesday.

The same people would show up week after week. Over time, I got to know their styles and personalities. One such person was the high-end interior decorator who acquired Rosenthal crystal and porcelain for her clients and requested that I put aside any that came in and call her.

"I'm curious about something," I once said to her as I was wrapping one of the eight pieces she had bought that day. "Why Rosenthal?"

"It's highly recognizable among my clients," she explained.

"Why?" I asked, looking at the golden scrolls and swirls on the cake plate I was about to wrap.

"Turn that over," she told me.

I carefully flipped the porcelain over onto the tissue paper. The mark on the bottom had two names: Rosenthal and Versace.

"Not many people know about this partnership," she smiled. "But my clients know. And their friends know. What they don't know is that I acquired this for $39.99 and I'll sell it to them for $175. And they will still think it's a bargain."

For a second, I was angry, incensed that she was ripping off her clients. But I realized she was running her business. I did some quick mental math, calculating her markup at more than 300%. It was no different than Wal-Mart selling me a pair of $15 flip flops that cost the behemoth $3, a 400% markup.

People love a bargain, but designers who can re-sell their bargains at a huge profit or who can stage a home with the most unique flair are the ones that showed up faithfully. This was a vital part of their businesses.

There are some designers who have the capacity to warehouse furniture. These are people who have been designing homes for years. They know what their clients will want and can easily take a risk on buying something a year or two before it becomes trendy. These designers will also rent their furnishings and accessories to stagers.

There are stagers who also have the capacity to store items. I used to imagine a warehouse filled to the rafters with miscellaneous items, but in actuality, stagers typically use storage lockers. The most Chatty Kathy of the stagers I knew, whose name really was Kathy, told me she rented three medium-sized storage lockers.

"Isn't that expensive?" I asked as we loaded her most recent purchases into her minivan.

"It's cheaper than having a warehouse," she answered.

"How much furniture can you fit in one of those?"

"Enough for a 4,000-square-foot house."

I was impressed.

"How do you keep track of what you have?"

"I'm organized," she shrugged. "Two of my lockers hold a particular style of furniture. An entire house in one locker. The third houses all the accessories. Want to see them one day?"

I did, but never followed up on the invitation.

"How often do you refresh what you have?"

"Every few years. Or sooner, if the buyer of the new home wants to keep all the furnishings."

"Does that ever happen, for real?"

She nodded. "Yup. I've been staging for almost a decade and it's happened three times. Of course, that depends on the colour of the year."

Prior to my time at HomeSense, I was blissfully ignorant of Pantone's colour of the year, which is announced every December. This colour, nuanced by culture, global mood, and trends, becomes insanely relevant for designers. The day I learned about Pantone's colour of the year, I drove up to the store just before 7 a.m. and discovered four human forms huddled in thick parkas waiting outside the doors. It was freezing, with light flakes of snow floating like seeds from a fluffy white dandelion. I paused before I got out of my car, unsure if it was safe to get out. Was I about to be mugged or murdered? It's not an overreaction. It's retail.

As I opened my car door, a face wrapped in a faux fur hood turned in my direction. It was Kathy. I didn't see the faces of the other three, whose chins were buried inside the necks of their parkas.

"Good morning," I sang. "What brings you out here so early? Kind of frigid to be lining up for discounted wall art."

"It's Pantone day," Kathy explained, through chattering teeth.

"What's Pantone day?" I asked, sliding my store key into the lock, turning it until I heard the barrel click open.

"It's the day we find out what the colour of the year will be." She was bouncing on her toes. I suspected it was both the cold and the excitement. "We need to be ready to get everything in that colour."

"What time do they announce?"

"Sometime this morning. Usually before 9 a.m."

"I wish I could invite you inside, but…"

"That's okay." Kathy smiled. "Larissa is coming with coffee and hot chocolate and then we'll take turns warming up in her van."

The store didn't open until 9:30 a.m. I couldn't imagine being in that frigid air for so long. As I opened the front door, warm air puffed out of the vestibule. I felt guilty walking into the store, leaving these people outside.

As I disabled the alarm and prepared the back room to receive new goods, I thought about the designers. They were a fiercely competitive group, but they staked their territory with class and composure. Unlike the women fighting over sweaters at Gap, this group was respectful of each other, even though they were all swimming in the same pool. When one grabbed a stellar accessory, the others voiced their jealously while simultaneously complimenting the victor on her acquisition. It was the most civilized behaviour I had seen in my years in retail.

I was oblivious when the announcement happened, elbow deep in receiving inventory with the staff, moving the goods down the conveyor belt to the rolling carts we used to bring the stuff to the sales floor. I sliced my finger open that morning when I reached into a box and grabbed hold of a shard of a ceramic figurine. Broken ceramics will serrate through layers of skin like a great white shark's teeth through seal flesh.

"Cute move," one of the designers said, nodding toward my finger, now wrapped in paper towel stained with blood.

The confusion must have been clear on my face.

"Colour of the year is True Red," Kathy said as she whizzed by me, pushing her shopping cart toward throw pillows.

By noon, the store was devoid of anything red. The latecomers left empty-handed, while those who froze their asses off reaped the rewards. I learned that in home decor and design, it didn't matter if the kitchen utensils, throw blankets, vases, wall art, lampshades, or decorative soaps were True Red. It mattered that they were red, period.

Most of us wouldn't know the difference between True Red (2002), Chili Pepper (2007), or Marsala (2015).

Most of us don't even know Pantone exists, let alone that it will determine how we paint our walls or choose our clothing. As a merchandiser, I started to pay attention to Pantone and the colour of the year from that point on. I read the information the company posted on their website, outlining the emotional impact of the colour as well as the usage guidelines. I probably knew more about the Pantone colour of the year than any other retail manager I had ever worked with or would work with in the future. It was my secret weapon, one that enabled me to become a kick-ass merchandiser who built displays—against company planograms— that did exactly what I wanted them to do: generate interest and sell shit.

20

Aisle Shopping

My next management job was also at a large home goods store, Home Outfitters, an offshoot of the Hudson's Bay Company. There were no discounts here. Rather, there was a lot of high-end merchandise sealed behind glass. It was in this store that I discovered one could spend $15 or $300 on a frying pan. I learned to tell the difference between a paring knife and a deboning knife. I felt the difference between 300-thread-count and 600-thread-count Egyptian cotton (the latter is lovely, but requires more care and I will never iron my sheets). I was hired as the human resources and front-end manager, where I would spend the bulk of my work day tucked into an office in the back of the store. If I so chose, I could spend my entire day off the sales floor, with the exception of having to cover a cashier's bathroom break or handle a complaint at customer service.

That's not how I roll. I like being with people. I took

the job because the money was good and I had the opportunity to learn a new side of retail management.

When my HR training was complete and I was assigned to a store, I asked my store manager, Kim, if I could get some training on the floor.

"Why?" she asked, clearly perplexed.

"I'd like to see how each department works. What the popular items are. What's important for me to know."

She furrowed her brow. "But those things aren't really relevant to your job. You need to do *your* job. Focus on that."

Kim was abrupt and cold. She delivered criticism without emotion and was stingy with praise. She was miserable and harsh. From a corporate perspective, retail management was the perfect career choice for her. She liked structure and had laser-focus on the bottom line. She ruled with an iron fist and was extremely inflexible. Compassion was not one of her personality traits.

In a brief flash of brilliance, I knew what I had to say to get some time on the floor.

"Since I'm new here, I'd like to assess the employees. See who is performing and who isn't. If I have the full-timers show me how they do their jobs, I'll be able to see who is ready for the next step. I assume succession planning is a human resources function."

I didn't know if that was true, but I was taking a gamble that having employees ready to move into management was something on which a store manager was measured. In every store I worked in to date, the annual assessment for GMs included a line item for succession. Bonuses were often awarded for every future manager who was groomed and promoted.

She looked at me long enough to make it uncomfortable. I was hoping for a smile, but what I got was a nod of the head.

"Okay. One day per week. And it can't be on Mondays."

Mondays were payroll processing days. I had to manually check time cards with hours logged into the system, correct errors, fix payroll mistakes from the previous period, and run reports Kim could use to report to head office in her weekly calls.

When I took over the human resources office, I inherited a godawful mess of a system. My predecessor went on maternity leave and never came back, an irony that would soon become clear. The sales manager, Andrew, was saddled with a job he knew nothing about. On my first day in my office, every single employee working that day knocked on my door. I thought it was nice they were coming to introduce themselves, so friendly and eager to meet the new manager. After the introduction though, I was assaulted with anger and frustration. Every single one of the eight full-time employees had missing pay and miscalculated holiday pay, and were stewing about annual raises that were not being paid.

"How long has Andrew been on HR?" I asked Kim.

"Three months," she answered. *Okay*, I thought, *three months is only six payroll periods. I can fix that.*

"But no one did anything in there for three or four months after Lorna left."

I was both horrified and excited by the challenge ahead of me.

"Good luck," Kim said with a smirk and walked away.

There was no way I was going to get on the sales floor until everything was fixed. Learning how each department was functioning was nowhere near as important as fixing payroll. You don't fuck with people's money.

Inside my office, a tall and wide filing cabinet was pushed up against one wall. Each of the four drawers was filled with folders and papers all piled one on top of the other. *Who was Lorna and how did she not know how to use hanging file folders?* I was going to have to clean up the mess before I could clean up the mess.

Employee folders were in random piles in all drawers. Hiring packages were spread out all over the place. In the top drawer I found the tax forms every employee had to fill out; in the bottom drawer was the employee information form where they filled out name, address, and emergency info. I randomly pulled out an employee's folder and went through the contents. I didn't need to know whose file I was looking at to know there was paperwork missing. The next folder I picked up was similarly in disarray.

I was facing a gargantuan task, but I knew I could piece everything back together like a puzzle fresh out of the box. I created a checklist of all the documents that had to be in every employee's file and worked from there.

It took me two months to sort everything out, organize the filing cabinets, and fix all the payroll issues.

"Did you know that there are employees still in the system who haven't worked here for a year?" I asked Kim.

"Didn't know, don't care. It's your job to handle these things."

"You should care," I fired back. "Until I removed them from payroll, some ex-full-timers were still getting benefits and statutory holiday pay. This was coming off the bottom line. Now that it's fixed, your bonus should be better."

I smiled, very pleased with myself for putting the last piece into the puzzle.

"Make sure it never happens again," she huffed.

For the first time in my life, a terrible four-letter word swept through my brain when I was talking to another woman.

But she was the boss, and it wasn't smart for me to challenge her or push back. She clearly didn't care about my good work, nor did it even occur to her that I had inherited someone else's mess.

"Oh, by the way," I called after her, "we don't have anyone assigned to the bridal registry."

She stopped, turned, and walked back to me.

"That's my baby," she told me. "I take those appointments. Only me."

"What if someone books an appointment on your day off?"

"I come in and take care of it."

I hadn't seen her ever come in on her day off, but truthfully, I had been so buried in cleaning up the HR chaos, I really had little idea of what was happening on the sales floor. I couldn't understand why Kim was so possessive of the bridal registry. More often than not, bridal registries were filled with abandoned items. Brides and grooms came into the store, selected all the things they wanted and needed for their married life and we built the list. I knew from my own registry that not everything was purchased. There was a good chance you'd get four of the eight place settings of the good china you wanted. You were for sure going to get all the everyday drinking glasses, and if the registry wasn't properly updated, you could end up with 40 water glasses and two wine goblets. It was an imperfect system, with no guarantee of sales for the store. It made zero sense for a store manager to take ownership.

It was my full-time cashier, Jenna, who filled in the gap for me.

"She's shopping," she said.

"For what? Bed linens?"

Jenna laughed. "Kim only dates married men. You knew that, right?"

The shock on my face clearly let her know that I didn't. I knew Kim was dating someone she complained about frequently. In the back offices, I heard her whining to the merchandise manager about how her boyfriend was emotionally unavailable but she was thrilled he was able to escape with her for a weekend. I never clued in that he was unavailable because he was married to someone else.

"She's making lists and taking names," Jenna said. "She's shopping for her next boyfriend."

21

The Final Climb

"**I** need you to check that all the towels are labelled," Kim said to me as soon as I walked into the store. "Grab a price gun and meet me in bed and bath."

I had arrived 15 minutes early for the start of my shift, intending to sip my coffee while I caught up on emails and started processing payroll. Kim had other plans. I knew if I didn't drop my things and race to the sales floor, she would berate me later. She operated in her own bubble, completely oblivious to what was happening around her, making demands that were unreasonable. But in retail, you can't complain. When you do, you're labelled as not being a team player.

I took a few gulps of my coffee, burning the roof of my mouth, before leaving it behind in my office. I greeted some associates on my way to the towels, flashing a bright smile that I hoped let them know I was on their side.

"She's on a warpath," Jenna whispered to me as I

passed her. Her arms were loaded with boxes of the tissue paper we used to wrap the fragile items people purchased. I stopped to help her, but she shook her head.

"Just go. I'm okay." I didn't argue. She had worked with this woman for more than five years. I had been at the store for thirteen months.

When I arrived at bed and bath, Kim was knee-deep in towels she had piled on the floor.

"What's up?"

"All these linens need to be checked for price tags. If they don't have them, print them," she ordered, shoving the price gun in my hand. "Inventory starts next week."

"What about payroll? It's due at noon."

She looked around the department. She examined the piles she had left on the floor and the wall of folded towels. Her eyes were everywhere but on me.

"Work fast, then," she snapped before walking away.

Tears sprang to my eyes. I was emotional for a big reason: I was eight weeks pregnant. I was keeping it to myself, following the "12 weeks until you tell" rule. For a moment, I had considered telling Kim about the pregnancy, before I realized it wasn't relevant to the work I had to do.

I kneeled on the floor, checking each bath towel, hand towel, and washcloth for price tags. I printed tags as I went, working quickly through the wall and the fixtures. After three hours in linens, my clothes were covered in bits of cotton. I had price tags stuck to my knees. I had one hour to process payroll, a job that normally required at least two and a half.

I submitted the last numbers just before noon. I said a silent prayer to the payroll gods that I hadn't screwed anything up in my haste to make the deadline. I was making my way to the front of the store to go out for lunch when Kim stopped me.

"Did you finish?" she asked.

I nodded. "All the towels are done."

"What about the shower curtains and bath accessories?"

"I… I didn't know you wanted those done."

She pursed her lips and squinted her eyes. Now it was my turn to let my eyes wander. I squirmed under her withering gaze.

"What did you think I meant when I told you check for tags in bed and bath?"

I racked my brain to recall our earlier conversation. I was sure she had only asked me to tag towels. *Did I hear her wrong? Maybe I already have pregnancy brain.*

"That section needs to be completed before you leave today."

As she walked away, heading toward the offices at the back of the store, I turned toward the front doors. I was starving and I measured the risk of not eating versus the risk of not finishing the task. It struck me as ridiculous that I even had to consider making a choice between my job and my baby. Of course I chose baby.

Taking a 30-minute lunch break wouldn't set me back horribly in the task ahead, but I had no idea the physical toll skipping a meal might take on my baby-building body. I bought a salad at the nearby grocery store and sat at one of the tables in their makeshift café, taking enough time to chew. I didn't go back to the store; I didn't want Kim running interference, leaving my salad to wilt next to my cold, congealed coffee.

Back at the store, I was fully focused on getting the work done. I put in 14 hours that day and went home with sore legs and knees and a level of exhaustion I didn't know was possible. When I told Jeff I had almost fallen asleep at the wheel on my drive home, he decided from then on he would be driving me to and from work.

Inventory is exhausting work for the store employees and managers who do the counting. Every item must be accounted for: every fork, every facecloth, every bag of decorative beads must be handled and scanned. Items that are part of a display are counted beforehand and labelled with Do Not Inventory (DNI) tags. Depending on the size of the store, inventory can take three to four days to be completed. The inventory team descends on the store in the evening, usually an hour or so before closing. The inventory company manager meets with the store managers to build a plan for where to start and how to manage items that have no tags or don't scan properly. The work happens overnight. Over the course of inventory, it's typical for a manager at every level to work 50 hours over three days.

"You have to tell Kim you're pregnant," Jeff told me the next morning as he drove me to the store for 6 a.m. "She has to know what your limitations are."

He was right, but I was afraid to open my mouth. This woman spat venom with every word. I had already complained about her to corporate human resources when she abandoned me in the store for six hours without a break and scheduled me to work back-to-back shifts despite the labour laws stipulating an eight-hour break between shifts was required. "She's not the worst manager you could have," the corporate representative claimed. "She's actually one of the easiest to work with."

As I unfolded myself from the car, Jeff gently encouraged me to stand my ground.

"This is our baby. You can always find another job." A supportive partner is vital when you work in retail. My first husband would have told me to suck it up and keep my mouth shut.

I opened the store, fired up the systems, and reviewed the plan Kim had left in the management office. Today, I was planning on tackling table linens. Placemats were the most notorious for not having labels since they tended not to stick well to the fabric and plastic. I was looking forward to a few hours of mind-less tagging as I went through 200-plus placemats.

Kim arrived 20 minutes after I did. Since we were alone, I took the opportunity to share my news.

"Kim, I want to let you know that I'm eight weeks pregnant."

Her eyes immediately went to my belly. She frowned for a second before she caught herself and smiled with her lips pressed together.

"Congratulations. When are you due?"

"August."

She nodded her head, then walked out of the office. I wasn't sure if she wanted me to follow her or if I needed to give her any more information about what was safe for me until I passed the 12-week window. Perplexed, I went back to my office to take care of some outstanding scheduling and payroll issues I needed to attend to.

When the rest of the management team and the employees scheduled to work that day were all in the store, Kim held our morning meeting. She let everyone know what their assigned duties were for the day: sales floor, cash desk, returns and recovery, and inventory.

"Dana, you'll be on bedding today. The high shelves need to be cleaned and checked for pricing."

My mouth hung open. Surely she was not going to send me up a ladder, digging into the upper reaches of our shelving units to check prices. I thought it was common knowledge that during the first three months of pregnancy, it was advisable to avoid anything strenuous or stressful. I couldn't evade stress, but the strenuous part seemed easy to control.

Once everyone had dispersed, I approached Kim to ask for a safer assignment. My palms were sweating and I was as nervous as if I was asking for a raise. Take note: if talking to your boss makes you feel like you're going to upchuck your vending machine granola bar, start looking for another job. A great leader will never make you feel that way.

Kim had her head down in some reports as she headed to the back office.

"Um, Kim," I said to her back, "can I talk to you for a second?"

She whipped around, and I could read the annoyance in every line of her middle-aged forehead.

"Can this wait?" she snapped. "I have a lot to prep before the inventory team arrives tonight."

"Um… well… it's just…." My armpits joined the sweat party that had begun in my palms. My grape-sized baby flip-flopped in my stomach. Jeff's voice drifted into my head. *Tell her. For our baby. It's just a job.*

"I can't get up on a ladder," I blurted out. "My blood pressure can change quickly because I'm pregnant and…"

Kim cut me off. "This is part of the job. If you can't do your job, maybe you shouldn't be here."

She stormed off, making it very clear the conversation was over. Fighting back tears, I walked over to bedding, examining the rolling ladder from the floor to the highest point. With a lump in my throat and my heart hammering in my chest, I began the climb. At the halfway point, five steps up and three feet off the ground, my head started to swim. Anxiety kicked in and the sweat moved again, this time from my pits to the nape of my neck. A single trickle rolled into the collar of my company-issued polyester shirt. I wasn't going to be able to do this. Pre-pregnancy, I loved getting up on the ladder. The platform elevated me seven and a half feet off the ground, giving me a bird's-eye view of the store. The structure was solid and I never once felt unsafe. Until this moment. Now, fear overwhelmed me. I held the tears back, slowly climbing down. In my office, I sank down in my chair and called Jeff at work, hiccupping my sentences between the tears.

Jeff picked me up within 30 minutes. I barely acknowledged Kim as I walked out of the store.

"I'm not feeling well," was all she deserved to know.

Later that afternoon, my gynaecologist squeezed me in for an emergency appointment. By the time Jeff came to pick me up, my stomach was cramping and I was having trouble breathing. I sat on the exam table and told my doctor about what had transpired at work that morning. Without hesitation, she wrote me a note, diagnosing preeclampsia.

"Some women just turn on their pregnant peers," she told me. "I see this all the time in workplaces, especially when the boss is a woman. It will only get worse later in your pregnancy. Best you get out now and grow this baby in a safe environment."

I couldn't believe that women would treat each other with such contempt. On the drive back to our condo, I was imaging how it would go when I went back to the store, letter in hand, telling Kim I was taking early leave. Part of me was terrified of the confrontation, but the other part of me was relieved.

The next morning, I dropped Jeff off at work, then went to the store. It was weird going in there, having walked out the day before. It didn't escape my notice that Kim hadn't even followed up with me to see how I was.

I found Kim in the bedding department, up on the ladder I refused to climb.

"My doctor has put me on medical leave," I told her.

She looked down at me, a look of panic passing over her face. She was calculating how she would manage my absence.

"Effective immediately," I said before she could utter a word. I had my doctor at my back, my partner's support, and this was not open for discussion.

"I'll put the letter on your desk."

She called out to me to wait as I walked away, but I didn't stop. In the office, I said a quick goodbye to my colleagues without explanation, dropped the letter on the clutter of Kim's desk and walked out of the store. That was my last day in retail.

22

Release Without Recidivism

I was still nestled in the warmth of our bed when Jeff kissed me goodbye the next morning.

"This is the right thing," he assured me.

The night before, all my fears about how I left the store bubbled to the surface. I was nervous about how we would survive financially. I was anxious about a stain on my reputation. I had worked so hard, always trying to climb the corporate ladder, moving from company to company in search of a career, and now, I was out of it. Kim would make sure there was nowhere for me to advance if and when I decided to return to work.

For the first time in 10 years, I had nowhere to go. There was no rush to do anything. This was a totally different feeling from a day off, when I usually had a laundry list of errands. I had eight months to spend reflecting on what I had been chasing and why.

When I first stepped into the retail management world, I was barely an adult. At 28 years old, when I was offered my first management position, I thought retail was beneath me. I had two university degrees. Surely that entitled me to a better career path.

I definitely had delusions of grandeur. From my first day at Chapters, I learned that just because your contract had "manager" typed somewhere in the sea of words, you were not the captain of the ship until your employees said you were. I had to earn the respect of the people who worked for me. I figured out early in my career that in order to be a successful leader, you had to be prepared to take shit even if it wasn't yours. If I directed someone to do something and they messed up, it was my fault for not communicating clearly. If I failed to give the people on the sales floor proper instructions, I took the fall when head office demanded to know why the new merchandise was still in the back. In the midst of the lessons, I was hurt, both emotionally and professionally.

I made the erroneous assumption that doing my job better than expected would earn me a coveted promotion to head office. As a self-starter, I took risks that I hoped would be good for the company. I accepted reprimand when I failed, but pushed back against the criticism when I succeeded. Why was I being written up for using prime sales floor real estate to display high-end enamel cookware when I sold 1,400 units in 12 hours? I held on to the hope that someone, somewhere in the company would notice that even though that wasn't the way things were supposed to be done, my decision generated more than $100,000 in sales in a single day. But in reality, that never happened.

This was the one lesson I took a long time to learn: in retail, breaking the rules, even when the outcome is overwhelmingly positive, is never rewarded. When I acted with the belief that what I was doing was good for the store or for my staff, I never stopped to consider that I'd be stepping on someone else's toes or making an executive look like a fool. Am I the asshole for acting with benevolence while trying to reach new heights in my career? To this day, my answer remains the same: fuck no.

My release from retail allowed me to sit in my room and think about what I had done, like I did when my mother punished six-year-old me. During the 240 days I waited for our son to be born, I replayed scenarios in my mind, wondering how I could have done things differently and trying to determine if altering my choices would have had better outcomes. Again, my answer was fuck no.

I eventually came to the conclusion that I wasn't built for a life in retail management. I would always make decisions in favour of the customers and the staff, despite direction from my superiors. My moral compass was too strong to stay silent when fellow managers were doing things they shouldn't and that had put nails in my career coffin. I wasn't willing to compromise myself for the promise of a promotion that might never come because I'm *not* an asshole. I was—and still am—a brilliant merchandiser, someone who is willing to speak out, and, most importantly, a human being with feelings. Only one of those things would serve me in retail, but the other two would keep me from returning.

For the first few weeks I was off, I spent countless hours in front of the computer, playing Bejeweled and checking my priorities. As the months ticked by, I felt the toxicity of the retail world leaving my mind and my body. While my belly swelled, my shoulders relaxed and my mind was at ease. My extended maternity leave turned out to be healthy for me too. Despite not knowing what the future held, financially and professionally, I felt free. I was done fighting. There would be no recidivism for me.

23

Returns

More than a decade after I left the retail management world, I was standing in line for the returns at Costco. At any time of day, this is a very long line. Costco has a reputation for having a very lax return policy. As a consumer, I appreciate that immensely, but whenever I buy anything there, I have to take the return line wait into consideration. I've seen the line extend to such a degree that the returnees blend in with the people making their way out of the store. I once drifted into the wrong line, getting frustrated about how slow it was getting out of the store. My fries with gravy were getting cold. I was standing in a sea of waving receipts, unable to tell for a good seven minutes that I was in the wrong line. I should have noticed the lack of shopping carts in my line, but I was hungry and not capable of using sound judgement.

As I stood in line (the proper one this time) waiting to return some clothes I had bought for my kids, my eyes wandered, assessing what the people in front of me were hoping to return. The returns line has always been an interesting storyline for me. My writer mind wanders, creating stories around the items being brought back. The odder items whipped my brain into overdrive, making up stories I would never write. The man with the winter boots bought an RV and decided to winter in Mexico. The mom with twin babies in a stroller is so addled she forgot she already bought those pyjama sets. The woman returning the bag of popcorn is dating someone with an irrational fear of foods that are choking hazards and she really wants this relationship to work.

The man now at the front of the line had a golf bag filled with clubs. The bag was grass-stained, and the clubs bore strike marks from where the balls had met the metal heads. It was late October, clearly the end of the golf season. The half dozen people in front of me in line watched this return unfold with great interest.

"Hi, what are you returning today?" the clerk asked, pretending she didn't see the golf bag the man was shuffling on the floor in front of him.

"I'm returning these golf clubs."

"And the bag?"

"Yeah, it's a set."

"Do you have the receipt?"

"No."

"Okay. Membership card, please."

Costco does not need receipts for returns. All your purchases are tracked and attached to your card.

She scanned the card, studying the screen, looking for the transaction.

"You bought these in March…"

"That sounds right, yes."

"… of last year," she finished.

Even from as deep into the line as I stood, I could see this associate really wanted to break the "No Questions Asked" return policy. Her eyes narrowed for a brief second before she caught herself. She smiled as she walked around from behind the counter to retrieve the set that had been used for two golf seasons. She processed the refund without another word. The only items deemed final sale at Costco are alcohol and cigarettes.

Having been on the other side of that counter, I have a good idea what happens to the returns. Clothing generally ends up back on the sales floor to be re-sold if the labels are still intact and there's no evidence of washing or wearing. Perishables and food items are discarded. Appliances, especially the small ones, will be put back on the shelf if the customer says they never even opened them. If they report it didn't work, it will be put aside into the RTV—return to vendor—pile, a returned items dumping ground. Most large companies negotiate RTV terms that favour the retailer, not the wholesaler. I've heard vendors say they have no choice but to agree to the terms if they want to sell their goods. One vendor shared with me their contract stated that not only did the big retailer have the right to send back everything for full credit, but the vendor had to cover the costs of shipping said items back to them. The vendor had to make arrangements for that shipping to happen every 60 days or pay a storage fee to the retailer.

Working for a store that had kinder arrangements with its vendors, I saw exactly how returns were handled. In our stockroom, a skid pallet sat in the corner with a large empty cardboard box sitting on top. The pallet was four feet long and four feet wide. The box fit the dimensions and rose to almost three feet high, high enough to toss things in, but too awkward to reach in and take things out. Someone, often me, would handwrite a sign with the vendor's name and tape it to the side of the box. This let the staff know what items would go inside and every return of a product from that vendor was put into that box. Every 60 days, the box would be wrapped with plastic off a roll, a task that required the finesse of a prima ballerina. One misstep and the clingy pallet wrap would stick to the wrong place or bunch up or tear. And because things were tossed willy-nilly into the soft-sided cardboard box, we had to wrap the pallet tightly to account for shift. Wrap it too loose, and all the items inside would shift and likely cause the cardboard box to tear open and spill its contents while in transit. Wrap it too tight, and the items inside would be squeezed like a pimple ready to pop—which it would undoubtedly do the moment we tried to move the pallet.

Among the unbelievable returns I have witnessed from either side of the counter were:

- A garden fountain that was left outside all winter, causing the hoses to crack. The customer expressed his frustration with the quality of the statue. From where I stood in line, I could see the photo pasted to the box of a kneeling woman, holding an urn, pouring water into a small pond. I thought he was lucky the whole thing had not cracked apart. I may have muttered "Hell no" when he presented the cashier with the woman's head.

- Used underwear. I can't even.

- Big screen TVs brought back the day after the Super Bowl. Go to Costco on the Monday after the big game, get a hot dog and a pop, and watch the steady stream to the returns desk.

- Toddler jeans that had holes worn into the knees. When offered a replacement pair, the customer requested a pair that was two sizes larger. I'm not ashamed to say I was filled with glee when I told her we could only exchange the well-loved denim for the same size. My bubble was burst when another employee told me the customer would likely just take the new jeans to another store and exchange them for a new size.

- Half-eaten Christmas and Thanksgiving turkeys and hams that the customer took the time to dress, cook, and carve. That's one way to deal with the leftovers, I guess.

- Two dead leaves in a Ziploc bag allegedly from a tree purchased at a nursery. The customer had his receipt, but was denied the

refund. He presented leaves from an ash but
his receipt indicated he had purchased a
ficus. A glorious win for the arborists.

I'm continually amazed with the creative ways people attempt to mask what they're returning. Until I worked in housewares, I was just as frustrated as anyone when I attempted to put a small appliance back in its box to return. I now suspect this is intentional, to make it more difficult for people to return items. But there are people skilled enough to put everything back into the box without any bulges or missing styrofoam. The sealing tape has been opened and resealed with such skill, it truly looks like the box was never opened. A friend of mine bought what she thought was a brand new Vitamix, only to discover it was used, with bits of unidentifiable food glued to the blades. Yes, people will return used small housewares without attempting to even clean them first.

When I was a teenager, stores were not so forgiving or generous with their return policies. I chose not to shop at stores that had a "No Refunds" policy. Back in the 1980s and 1990s, store credit was usually issued and employees were instructed to encourage that before giving any money back. Somewhere along the line, the policies changed to favour the customers. I'm okay with that. Retail is a symbiotic relationship between corporation and consumer. We cannot survive without each other. A few bad apples can spoil the whole barrel, but there will always be people who game the system and take advantage of it. I'm thankful for those patrons because they left me with stories to tell.

Early in my retail career, I worked for a short period of time in a neighbourhood grocery store. It was an eye-opening experience on many levels. I learned about food spoilage and just how much produce ended up in the trash. I saw people open boxes of crackers or bags of chips to eat a handful and then put the item back on the shelf. I watched as customers put their hands in the bulk bins to take samples, like they were at an all-you-can-eat buffet. When I was presented with my first-ever return at the cash register, I was a bundle of nerves. People tended to yell when they didn't get their way.

"I'd like a refund for this tin of coffee, please."

"Is there anything wrong with it?"

"It tastes like dirt."

"Uh, okay. Do you have a receipt?"

"No. I threw it out."

My stomach fluttered. The store policy was to issue store credit when there was no receipt. I was barely a teenager and I was not good with confrontation.

"I… uh… um… I can only, uh, give you, like, store credit," I stammered, keeping my eyes on the coffee sitting on the counter. Internally, I braced myself for her anger.

"Can I just exchange this for something else? A different brand?"

"I… I guess so." I lacked any confidence to make that kind of decision. "But let me check with my manager."

I called him from the back office and he told me to process the return and the sale in the same transaction.

"What if the new coffee is less than the return?" I asked.

"Then offer a store credit. If she says no, and the difference is less than a few dollars, then she can have cash back." He hung up and my brain spun with more anxiety-driven questions. *What if the difference is more than two dollars and she won't take store credit? Do I tell her to add on some more things?*

I was anxious for nothing. The customer didn't make a big deal about the return, switching out the coffee for a different brand and buying a few more things she needed.

When I brought all the returns to the back—all returned food items were disposed of—I opened the can, curious about the coffee. As soon as I peeled back the plastic lid covering the top, the smell of earth filled my nostrils. Inside the can, the coffee was clumpy, not loose and grainy like I'd seen before. I stuck my nose further into the can, realizing that this was not coffee at all. It was no wonder it tasted like dirt: the can was filled with potting soil. The customer had switched out the coffee, proving once again there is really nothing people won't do to get their money back.

24

Receipts from a Pandemic

The coronavirus pandemic brought the plight of retail workers into full focus. For the first time, cashiers, stock people, and customer service associates were in the spotlight as "essential workers." Many grocery stores and drugstores gave their employees temporary raises as danger pay. I was glad for the attention on this typically ignored workforce, but also grateful that I was out of the game.

The nature of retail is such that we are always on the front line. We face the good and the bad, even when not in a pandemic. We've had people yelling in our faces and spraying their spit over a broken pot handle or a pair of jeans that shrank in the wash. We work back-to-back shifts, despite the law mandating how many hours' rest we need. But we also get to help people find the perfect gift, or teach them the difference between paring and boning knives.

The pandemic added a new layer of stress.

Customers were on edge, struggling with new rules and restrictions. But the employees were under their own excruciating level of stress.

The shy 17-year-old who was hired to stock the shelves was suddenly standing at the front door managing lines, telling people to wear their masks properly, and spraying everyone who came in with hand sanitizer. He wasn't trained to stand outside for his whole shift, not knowing when the next emotional explosion would happen in his face or how he was going to handle another fight among customers standing in line.

The young lady scanning your groceries is grateful for the mask hiding her fear. Her hands are dry and cracked from the plastic gloves she wears all day. She strips off her clothes in the garage before she comes into the house. As she throws her uniform into the washing machine, her hands go to her belly, cradling the baby she just found out is growing in there. She has no idea if this virus will affect her pregnancy, if her baby will be okay, if she will catch the virus and die. This is what she thinks about at the end of every eight-hour shift where she just earned $120 before deductions.

The greeter at the Wal-Mart, a senior citizen who took the job after retirement because he genuinely loves people and wanted to keep busy is terrified of getting sick and dying. He is somewhat relieved when, four months into the pandemic, he is laid off, replaced by a security guard who can handle the tension of the job better. He takes advantage of the early shopping hours at the grocery store, but the stress of lockdown is too much for him. He misses his recently deceased wife, but is glad she didn't have to live trapped inside their tiny condo, unable to see friends or family. This is not the retirement he imagined.

The stories of retail workers bled into the online world. There were videos of belligerent customers spitting on cashiers and yelling in the faces of managers about their rights and freedoms. Stores were continually hiring people to pick and pack grocery store orders for delivery or pick-up, replacing those affected by the virus. Every day was a symphony of emotions: fear of getting sick, relief for having a job as so many companies shuttered their doors, confusion about restrictions and having to deal with rules that changed from day to day, anxiety, loneliness, isolation, and helplessness on levels not seen outside of wartime. All behind newly installed Plexiglas barriers. All for minimum wage.

During the first year of the pandemic, the retail community fed us and protected us. Later, when stores selling non-essential goods started reopening, they were a place where we could frivolously spend the money we hadn't spent in the previous year. For 15 minutes, life could be a little bit closer to normal as we browsed for books or throw pillows or candles. Until restrictions started again.

There will always be a need for a retail workforce, even as more companies move to online sales. The pickers, the packers, and the delivery people are retail employees too.

Above all, they are people.

They have families, dreams, and bills to pay. They have lives outside of work. They have good days and bad days. They have bright ideas and imperfections. They get sick and they recover.

If I were still in the business, I hope I'd be at the level where I could fight on behalf of my employees. I was a horrible retail manager by corporate guidelines; I never cared about the bottom line or the margins. I cared about the people who did the work. I cared about the customers who chose to spend their money at my store. If I were a manager in the pandemic, I'd be out there with them, taking the risk of a customer coughing in my face, not hiding out of sight. These days, it's rare to see a manager on the floor helping customers, cleaning garbage, or doing any of the tasks they ask others to do.

Working in retail is a thankless job. The hours are long, the pay is garbage, and the working conditions are always less than ideal. For most, it's *just a job*. Very few people intentionally go into retail as a career choice.

The next time you hear someone berating a cashier, step in and say something. If you're not comfortable telling a fellow customer to cool it, take a moment to acknowledge the cashier when it's your turn. Thank them for the job they're doing. Apologize for the people who think it's okay to treat them like garbage. It can change the course of someone's day to show a little empathy.

I do not regret a single day I spent in retail, although at the time, I questioned my life choices on a daily basis.

For the better part of a decade, I was frustrated, lost, and belittled for less than $45,000 per year. I was stuck with no hope of moving up the ladder I so desperately thought I wanted to climb. I can say with certainty that if I had the chance to do it all over again, I would run screaming into the woods.

25

This Shit Really Happens

So many things happen in the retail environment on a daily basis, things that you'd think could only be fiction. *Superstore* is a funny television show because there is a great deal of truth in what is depicted.

The complaints from the sales floor haven't changed over the years. While I had hoped that woke culture would infiltrate the retail world, talking to current employees demonstrates this isn't the case. Part of the issue is the culture within retail from the corporate offices down to the part-time employees. The attitudes and expectations have gotten worse as the bottom line has become the sole purpose. Employees, including store-level management, are chattel, easily replaced by the next herd. Associates are still moaning about schedules: changes made without being notified, working the "Clopen" (closing the night before and opening the next morning), shifts being cancelled an hour before start. It's ironic to me that despite the internet putting all the information at our fingertips, people really don't know their rights, or even that they have rights at all. You have the right to be safe and free from discrimination in the workplace. Your employer cannot withhold your final paycheque. And you cannot be made to pay for shortages in the cash drawer if other people had access to it. Wherever you live, there are employment standards governing how your employer treats you.

On the other side of that coin is a glut of employees who don't value work. Even when I was a manager, there were always employees who called in sick when it was too late to replace them, or those who didn't show up and when I finally reached them told me, "Oh, sorry. I guess I forget to tell you my family went on vacation." There were some who took extended breaks and were surprised when they were dismissed. Stealing time is just as bad as stealing goods. I did have stellar, dedicated employees who wanted to work, who enjoyed showing up and wanted to learn how to be better at their jobs. Their reward was more shifts, but that meant I fielded many complaints from other staff who felt they were getting shafted. They were. And in the scheme of retail, giving—or not giving—them hours was the only measure of control I had. I didn't like firing people. I preferred the more gentle method of reducing their shifts until they found something else and quit.

The customers, however, have gotten worse. The sense of entitlement today is endemic. I don't have to be working in a store to witness the kind of behaviour that would shame an entire family. In my time, my biggest pet peeve was parents who let their children run around a store like it was a playground. They hid in racks of clothing, tried to climb the shelves, ripped open packages, spilled their hot chocolate/squeezed their juice box/smushed boxed raisins into and onto product. Even back then, long before I had my own children, I blamed the parents for not taking control. I can count *on one hand* how many times over more than a decade a parent apologized for their child's behaviour or offered to pay for the damages. Most of the time, the parent hustled the kids out of the store, away from the damage, with a glare to the manager who dared to say something to their children like, "Those shelves are not safe for climbing," or "Hangers aren't the best thing to put in your mouth."

When a six-year-old pulled all the pristinely folded T-shirts off a display table and buried himself, the mother threatened to sue us for endangering her child.

She was screaming, "He could have suffocated!" as the boy lay on the floor, burrowing into the pile and giggling.

"Mommy! Mommy! Look! I'm a mole in his hole!" She yanked him out by one arm and stormed out.

The patrons who stay in the store past closing are another sore spot. I have never had an issue with people wandering into the store five minutes before closing. If the sign says the store is open from 9 a.m. to 9 p.m., it's reasonable to expect to be able to shop anytime during that window. Every store will make closing announcements, letting the customers know the store is closing in 15, 10, or five minutes. The script varies little from store to store and always invites customers to check out any items they wish to purchase. I've had customers run into the store just as I start pulling the doors or gates closed, explaining they just need one thing.

"I'll be quick, promise!" And for the most part, they are.

I learned to be aggressive with those who wandered in to have a look around. I was on these people as soon as I saw them browsing without purpose.

"What can I help you find?" I always asked.

The answer was a variation of "Oh, nothing," or "I'm just browsing," or "I'll know it when I see it."

In the early days of my career, I would retreat, giving the customer all the time they needed. My employees were leaving, the cashiers closing off their tills. One person even took a pile of clothing into the fitting room, stood at the locked door and yelled, "Hello? Hello? Can someone come unlock these doors for me?"

I approached her, preparing myself for battle.

"I'm very sorry ma'am, but the store is closed."

"You weren't closed when I came in," she protested.

"True. But we closed 45 minutes ago. I had to let the staff go home."

She glared at me.

"Are you saying I can't try these on? That you don't want my money?"

I took a short breath through my nose, feeling very much like a bull about to charge. I pressed my lips together, then forced them into a thin smile.

"Ma'am, we do want your money. Unfortunately, the cashiers have all gone home and the cash register is closed. I'd be happy to take these items and put them on hold for you until closing tomorrow."

"Not good enough," she said, then dropped the entire pile of clothing at my feet and stormed away. My level of satisfaction deepened when seconds later I heard her again at the front gate.

"Hello? Is someone going to let me out?"

I sauntered to the front of the store, put my key into the mechanism on the wall, and watched her watching the gate rise slower than the sun from the horizon. When the gate had rolled three feet from the floor, she ducked underneath, her purse snagging on the bottom of the gate and she was almost pulled off balance.

"Thanks for coming in," I said to her back. She responded by giving me the finger.

For a moment, I wondered if she was a secret shopper. These are people hired to test your store, to make sure your employees are asking the customers the questions we've told them to ask, whether it's for an item of the week, an in-store credit card, or a simple, "Did you find everything you were looking for today?"

As a manager, I hated the secret shoppers. It felt like a betrayal to me, that my boss's bosses didn't trust us to do our jobs. The longer I spent in retail, however, the better I got at picking them out from the line, like the crappy undercover security you've passed four times in the grocery store and he still has only one item in his shopping cart. After my retail time was over, I became a secret shopper myself, spying on employees, then later sitting in the food court making my notes. I took this part-time job very seriously, memorizing my lines like a

Hollywood actress. Aside from the usual questions about sizes, returns, and contacting other stores for an elusive item, I had to say things like "This is way more than I wanted to spend," and wait for the employee to suggest layaway. My favourite was the retailer that instructed me to say, "I'm so clueless when it comes to putting outfits together," which was supposed to trigger the associate to say, "I can set you up with a personal shopper who can help. Can I book you an appointment?" The problem with this was most of the time, part-time employees didn't even know this service existed because their manager never communicated it. After a year, my conscience got the better of me and I stopped spying on people who were just trying to earn a living.

Not all retail is horrible. I was fortunate enough to be part of the opening teams for a casino, three bookstores, two clothing stores, and two homewares discount stores. It's exciting to be in the building before the store opens to the public. The energy is high every day despite the long hours of training, merchandising, and prep that takes place. When the doors finally did open, I was part of something special. The customers were curious, electrified, and animated. Something new is always a good thing.

With every store I opened, my hope was that things would be better. This time, I thought, the management team would support each other. This time there'd be no backstabbing. This corporation would allow us to focus on service to the customer, not the payroll percentages or sales numbers. And with every store opening, I rode the wave for a while. Until the bullshit and nonsense and corporate games started. And still, I stayed in the industry. I did love parts of it: engaging with people, watching the star employees rise, solving problems, helping that customer find the perfect gift. It was challenging and rewarding at the same time.

Way back when Greg, my regional manager at Gap, said we were just selling blue jeans, I agreed with him. But now? I think maybe we were doing way more than that.

Acknowledgments

I'd like to thank all the brilliant managers I've had the chance to work with and from whom I learned amazing things. There aren't that many, so I remember each and every one of you.

To all the crappy managers, I thank you too. You showed me how to never treat people. You gave me fodder for this book and inadvertently made me a better person. I'm still a crappy manager, in your eyes.

Thank you to Zoey Duncan, the best editor in the world. Once again, your input had proven valuable beyond measure. You ran this book in front of your weary new-mom eyes and still did not miss a beat. You are the best. Really. THE BEST.

To my husband, Jeff, and my boys, Mason and Westin: I know you get tired of hearing me talk about my writing, but you smile and nod because you love me. Also, I can see in your eyes that you're never quite sure if I'll turn my lens on you all in an over exaggerated, mostly true memoir about motherhood. I can't make any promises. I love you, forever and always.

About the Author

Dana Goldstein is the author of two other memoirs. Her first, The Girl in the Gold Bikini offers an examination of her journey through food and family. She has been known to cry over a sandwich offered to her after a harrowing event in Rome.

Her second memoir, Murder on My Mind, is a candid look at Dana's experience with perimenopause through to post-menopause. Within the pages, she discusses everything from murderous rages to the death of her libido.

She is also the author of two middle grade novels, and hosts a podcast, What Were You Thinking.

Dana lives in and writes from her home in Calgary, Alberta, Canada.

Find out more by visiting danagoldstein.ca

Also by Dana Goldstein

The Girl in the Gold Bikini

Murder on My Mind

CPSIA information can be obtained
at www.ICGtesting.com
Printed in the USA
BVHW081944200722
642001BV00003B/22